DATE DUE

The
Social
Network
Business
Plan

The Social Network Business Plan

290203

18 Strategies That Will Create Great Wealth

David Silver

WILEY

John Wiley & Sons, Inc.

√ Published by John Wiley & Sons, Inc., Hoboken, New Jersey
Published simultaneously in Canada

For general information on our other products and services or for technical support, please contact our Customer Care Department within the United States at (800) 762-2974, outside the United States at (317) 572-3993 or fax (317) 572-4002.

Wiley also publishes its books in a variety of electronic formats. Some content that appears in print may not be available in electronic books. For more information about Wiley products, visit our web site at www.wiley.com.

Library of Congress Cataloging-in-Publication Data:
Silver, A. David (Aaron David), 1941-
    The social network business plan : 18 strategies that will create great wealth/David Silver.
      p. cm.
  Includes bibliographical references and index.
  ISBN 978-0-470-41983-0 (cloth)
     1. Business planning. 2. Social networks. I. Title.
  HD30.28.S4344 2009
  658.4'01—dc22

                                                 2008037344

Printed in the United States of America

10 9 8 7 6 5 4 3 2 1

Contents

Acknowledgements

"WE ARE TALKING NOW OF summer evenings in Knoxville, Tennessee in the time that I lived there so successfully disguised to myself as a child," wrote James Agee, who was born and grew up about a block from my house in Knoxville, but a little before me. That's where I learned about communities: in Knoxville, chasing fireflies on summer evenings, while the adults from the various homes on our block sat drinking ice tea and lemonade on the back porch. We had a hobo in our neighborhood as well. His name was Nathan and he rolled a tire with a stick and talked to himself. All of the families on Third Avenue fed and clothed him. The problems of our community were solved by the community or they didn't get solved. Clogged sewers, broken street lamps, accumulating trash in the empty lots, an under performing teacher at Brownlow Elementary School, cars driving too fast . . . all of these issues were handled and done so very efficiently by the members of the community. It was all very informal but effective.

Now our world is more complex. People don't gather on back porches to solve shared community problems. They are isolated from one another. Some of the obvious solutions are blocked by regulation. Those three factors—*complexity, isolation,* and *regulation* —have been identified by entrepreneurs starting online communities and social networks as the three factors that pre determine a huge need for an online community or social network. As an angel investor for the last 30 years, I have always tried to catch waves, and the current wave I'm riding is the social network. Here's how I see the rolling of the waves. If there is no euphemistic back porch where the neighbors can meet to discuss and solve common problems, but rather the market is characterized by complexity, isolation, and regulation, I am probably going to see if I can find a strong entrepreneur to back in building a social network for that market.

There are other markers, such as the number of people who have the problem, the homogeneity of the problem, the price they will pay to solve it, and the willingness of the people with the problem to discuss it with others in the forum section of an online community. But, without complexity, isolation, and regulation, it probably will not be a wave I will fund with angel capital.

To be a wave-catcher, one needs outstanding helpers. And I have some wonderful support from Jennie Herrera, my executive assistant, and Susan Sterrett John, who manages our office. Other friends, advisors, and consultants who have contributed to both my wave-catching and this book include Bob Crull, Sylvan Corazzi, Kyle Gillman, Susan Mangiero, Gordon Dickson, Patrice Peyret, Robin D. Richards, Bob Armbrister, Claude Silver, Caleb Silver, Hank Carabelli, Ewan MacLeod, Sean Malatesta, Lynne Saccaro, Sheila Ortiz, Nancy Garcia, Diedre Adams, and Randy Farmer.

Special thanks to the Wiley team, and my editor, Shannon Vargo. As for my agent, Fredrica S. Friedman, who is *sui generis* in the field of publishing, I will say that it is an honor to be in her entourage.

—David Silver
Santa Fe, NM
October 2008

Introduction

HERE IS A ONE-SENTENCE DESCRIPTION OF THIS BOOK: There is a lot of money to be made if you get a lot of smart people talking and then sell their anonymized conversations to vendors.

That, in a nutshell, is what this book is about. Most of the text defines, describes, and elaborates on this sentence. It defines how all parties benefit. It describes how the money is made, by whom, who gets paid, how much is paid, paid to whom. Then it explains how you persuade a lot of smart people to start talking about something that has commercial value. What will they talk about? Why? When? Why will vendors pay to overhear these conversations?

I will explain all of this to you by defining an elegant new pain-solver called the *recommender online community*. *Online community* and *social network* are essentially the same thing, and I will use them interchangeably. The social network is a force of nature, that is, our natural inclination to join communities and associations in order to accomplish things that we cannot get done by acting alone. The recommender online community will create a new way to launch new products and services, and it will generate new revenue channels for old media. But it will also be enormously disruptive.

Disrupt the Old Business Model

There hasn't been a disruption machine as intrepid and force-ful as the recommender community since the invention of bread 6,000 years ago disrupted hunting and the preserving and eating of meat in the economic and social life of the inhabitants of earth. The existing model at the time was this: Find an animal, shoot the animal, cook it, and eat it. Then find another one. Then it all changed. Ants were seen by the Egyptians in 4000 B.C. sowing and reaping grass. According to Linnaeus, and echoed by Dr. Gideon Linceum, a nineteenth-century American physician, ants plant grass seeds around their mounds in the spring, harvest them in the fall, and take them inside their mounds, where they eat them in the winter.

While the men were out hunting, the women, who had observed the ants, began planting gardens. They invented a tool called the grubbing stick in order to dig furrows. In the furrows, the women dug holes and put grass seeds into the holes, then ran water through the furrows. The men came home from hunt-ing and observed the women, weary from work. They improved on the grubbing stick by tying a short stick to the end of a long stick to create the first plow. Then they created a harness for their cattle, attached the plow, and that enabled the women to make larger gardens, cultivate more grass, and produce more grain with which to make bread. Soon the men began participating in grow-ing wheat and making bread.

We know from the paintings in Egyptian pyramids that over time an industrial process evolved, along with municipal govern-ments, to build canals to distribute and store water from the Nile;

and we know that bread became the currency of Egypt and its trading partners for thousands of years. Nomadic societies, such as the Hebrews, and seafaring societies, such as the Greeks, had no ovens; and thus began commerce—the exchange of goods (fish) and services (slave labor) in exchange for bread.

Bread obtained religious significance. The cult of the bread goddess became the state religion of Athens. The Hebrews thanked Jehovah before eating their bread. And from the Bible, we know that the tempter came to Jesus and said, "If thou be the Son of God, command that these stones be made bread."

The disruptive effects that bread had on economic life six thousand years ago are being repeated today with the disruption of conventional business models by the recommender social network. The effects of bread on the hunter-gatherer economic life were these:

- People needed to form communities.
- The find-an-animal, kill-the-animal, bring-it-back-to-the-family, and go-out-and-find-another-animal business model was replaced by the wheat-growing community and its recurring revenue model, which was far less expensive.
- Bread (from wheat) became the currency of all civilization for thousands of years.

The corollary effects that recommender communities are having on economic life today are these:

- People feel the need to form review, rate, and recommend communities in order to find the truth about products and services, their prices and efficacy, the vendor's after-sale support, the best model and the worst one, and the experience that others have had with them.

- The find-a-customer-with-advertising, sell-the-customer-something, then-find-another-customer business model is being replaced with the recurring revenue model of recommender communities.
- Synthetic currency used in recommender communities will replace authentic currency.

Today the old revenue-generating model, which I call the "antelope hunt"—informs the customer with advertising, then goes out and catches the customer, sells something to the customer, then goes out and catches another customer—is dying, just as certainly as the hunting model was replaced by the bread model. Why so? Because placing ads on the Web to find new customers is completely wasteful. My ham sandwich can find a new customer on the Web faster than an advertisement can. So there will be a massive disruption as the antelope hunt model is replaced by sales influenced by recommender communities. Jobs will be lost in the four big support industries—advertising, marketing, sales, and public relations. All four will undergo massive layoffs followed by an Electra event to rise up once again in a new format.

The Efficiency of the Community Model

The management, stockholders, and employees of a company that sells a product or service spend a large part of the company's gross profit on advertising in order to find the customer and sell something to the customer. Then, having done that, they have to repeat the process. The managers meet with advertisers, the media, graphic designers, marketing consultants, lawyers, trade groups, lobbyists, foreign distributors, and others in order to improve the timeworn process of find a customer, sell something to the customer, then find another customer. This process is known as *shrinking the available market with each sale*. It is inefficient, costly, repetitive, and not conducive to innovation because of its centripetal, or inward-looking nature.

The recommender community, or for that matter, subscription-based businesses, are centrifugal in nature. It is a force that tends to impel its core content outward from the center of rotation. *When a subscription-based business sells a monthly pay membership to a customer, it expands its market by 11 consecutive payments.* Clubs like Netflix, franchising businesses such as KFC, party-plan sales organizations like Mary Kay Cosmetics, Internet service providers, and online communities and mobile social networks *expand their universes with each sale*. But the recommender community takes the franchising and subscription-based club model one giant step further—just as the ancient Egyptian men did when they took the plow out of the women's hands and attached it to their cattle—the members of social networks do the heavy lifting. They supply the need to collaborate with others, which is the *raison d'être* of the community's existence. The members supply the conversation. They create the value. They pay for minutes of connect time on their mobile phones to their Internet service providers. They provide the time to search for an inquiry of another member. And here is where the excitement comes in: *The old antelope hunter will pay through the nose to listen to anonymized conversations about products or services that are collected, sliced, diced, and bar-charted by the recommender community.* The recommender community business model is elegant and efficient, whereas the antelope hunt business model is clunky, costly, has too many moving parts, is less profitable, and ineluctably forces the consumers to pay more for the product or service. To feel its inefficiency first-hand, call Dell's customer service department and enter Dell Hell. CRM software has too many "thank you's" built into it and not enough real assistance.

There is a second market for the conversations and activities of the members of online communities: traditional media. Television, newspapers, and radio are dying. They need more advertising revenues. *The solution to their pain will be provided by online communities in the form of advertorials produced by the online communities and paid for by its "powered by…" sponsors.*

There are several more uses for the online recommender community. It is a good place to introduce new brands, and it is a good place to gain an endorsement. Ads will soon appear on products in retail stores that say, "Voted #1 by such-and-such social network."

Everyone benefits: Vendors learn what products are working and what products are failing—and the reasons why. Community members provide useful services and achieve their goals of better products and services and lower prices because they need less advertising for promotion. Old media captures new revenue channels. Retailers earn in-store ad revenue by placing "Voted #1" signs on some of their products. Communities take over the new product branding job. There are a lot of changes coming. But there will be blood.

Who Gets Disrupted and When?

The symbiotic service industries get disrupted most severely: advertising, marketing services, media, sales forces, public relations, shopping malls, and their supporting industries—printing, graphic arts, jingle writing, acting, and so forth. *The social networks, acting as consumer rating services or recommenders of products and services, will eliminate the need for finding the customer.* That task will become the principal task of the recommender communities. They will act like miter boxes, guiding the handsaw that is the consumer product or service, at the proper angle in making a miter joint between the product or service that the crowd of members want, at the price they want and delivered to them when they want it. If the members agree that a certain Procter & Gamble product can be trusted to absorb a baby's defecation without leakage, then Procter & Gamble will have found a recurring revenue stream without the need for massive advertising. Goodbye billions of dollars previously spent on advertising, marketing, eye-level shelf positioning, sales forces, media buying, and so forth. Hello increased efficiencies in the way consumer products and services are sold. The brilliant economic thinker and writer Peter Drucker said, "The purpose of marketing is to make selling easy." The social network that encourages reviewing, ranking, and recommending is the new marketing tool.

But if the community finds that the Procter & Gamble diaper is not as good as one being made by a start-up that uses stuffing similar to that used in Patagonia outerwear, or some other substance, such as the start-up MyLil Star, then goodbye Procter & Gamble's market share, because the recommender community will vote for the start-up. Baby care supplies were $6.5 billion in sales (at retail) in the United States in 2006, and diapers represent 69 percent of that figure. If the babyproductvotes.com community ranks Procter & Gamble's product near the bottom, it could lose billions of dollars in revenue, profits, and market capitalization. Marketplace power will shift to the consumers who belong to recommender online communities. Their power—oligopsony power—will be awesome, and the suits who work at the major brands will bend the knee and bow the head when dealing with them.

Oligopsony Power

What about oligopsony power? The advertising agencies, sales organizations, media companies, shopping center owners, supermarket chains, and acolyte industries will scream to their lawyers for forceful advocacy. Always ready for some billable hours, the lawyers will write useless briefs because they know that fear pays. But there is nothing illegal in forming associations in order to recommend and buy products more efficiently.

Hasbro, Inc., the owner of Scrabble's North American rights, sued Rajat and Jayant Agarwella, the developers of Scrabulous, in Federal Court on July 29, 2008. Facebook, which hosted the popular game played by millions of people, then removed Scrabulous; 46,000 people protested the removal of Scrabulous by Facebook in the first hour after it was taken down. Two days later it was reborn as *Wordscraper* with new rules and circular tiles. Thousands of people began playing the new game.

A few years ago, Sinclair Broadcasting and its advertisers felt the scorpion's sting of the collaborative power of smart people holding conversations. Sinclair reaches 26 million television-watching households. It is a decidedly pro-Republican company, and during the 2004 presidential elections, Sinclair decided it would broadcast a documentary called *Stolen Honor: The Wounds That Never Heal*, as a news program, ten days before the presidential election to embarrass John Kerry. The documentary "was reported to be a strident attack on candidate John Kerry's Vietnam War Service." The *Los Angeles Times* broke the story of Sinclair's plan a week before and alongside the standard Democratic responses, the blogosphere became rebarbative and agitated.

Josh Marshall on talkingpointsmemo.com, Chris Bower on MyDD.com, and Markos Moulitsas on dailykos.com launched "boycott Sinclair" messages. Their readers took up the baton and rebroadcast the boycott request throughout the Internet. Then, another blog, theleftcoaster.com, posted a variety of action agenda items, including picketing Sinclair affiliates, and dailykos. com published the names of the program's proposed advertisers. A reader of one of the blogs took matters into his own hands, got the list of local advertisers to an Ohio Sinclair affiliate, and organized a letter-writing campaign to its sales managers, saying they would boycott the local advertiser's products and services. He reported the success of his tactic on the blog. A boycott database of 800 advertisers was published on the blog, along with sample letters. A blogger picked up on this and wrote a program that he published on the Internet that instructed interested people on how to send the boycott letter to all 800 advertisers simultaneously. Sinclair's lawyers sent out threatening letters to everyone involved.

Then an analyst at Lehman Brothers issued a research report that downgraded the price of Sinclair stock, citing concerns about loss of advertiser revenue. Mainstream news reports picked up on the analyst's prediction, and Sinclair's stock price dropped 8 percent. The next day, the price fell another 6 percent, to its lowest point in three years. Sinclair pulled *Stolen Honor*.

The blog that contained the database of 800 advertisers received more than 300,000 unique visitors during its first week of operations and more than one million page views. And that was half a decade ago.

The Talisman of the Revolution

The revolution in the way goods and services are sold is a groundswell today. But it was predicted by Yochai Benkler, Harvard Professor of Internet and Ethics, in his 2006 landmark book, *The Wealth of Networks*, when he wrote, "A particular confluence of technical and economic changes is now altering the way we produce and exchange information, knowledge, and cultures in ways that could redefine basic practices." Forrester Research echoed Professor Benkler's promise when in November 2007 it wrote, "Seventy-one percent of online shoppers read reviews, making it the most widely read consumer generated content." And Bizrate in January 2008 said, "Fifty-nine percent of our users considered customer reviews more valuable than experts, reviews." James Surowiecki, author of the ingenious book, *The Wisdom of Crowds*, writes that "user-generated searches, stories, advertisements, designs, product reviews on many consumer products and services will nearly always be superior to those generated by a group of experts."

Trend spotters have reported such transformative events: "According to Global Nielsen survey of 26,486 Internet users in 47 markets, consumers' recommendations are the most credible form of advertising among 78 percent of the study's respondents" (www.bazaarvoice.com).

A consumer survey by the J.C. Williams Group ranked consumer content as the number-one aid to a buying decision (J.C. Williams Group, global retail consultants, October 2006).

Marketing Sherpa reports that "86.9 percent of respondents said they would trust a friend's recommendations over a review by a critic while 83.8 percent said they would trust user reviews over those of a critic" (Marketing Sherpa, July 2007).

BusinessWeek's cover story in its March 3, 2008, issue entitled "Consumer Vigilantes" reports that "behind the guerilla tactics is a growing disconnect between the experience companies promise and customers' perception of what they actually get." The article goes into detail about how *Advertising Age* editor Bob Garfield's blog, "ComcastMustDie.com," had a significant influence on improving Comcast's customer service.

Solving Pain

It is the task of the entrepreneur to solve pain. The pain that the recommender social network entrepreneur solves is to replace the gross inefficiencies of the current business model— which we see in the nonrecurring revenue model—with the efficiencies of the recommender social network. The recommender community will lower the price of all consumer goods and services by gathering consumers into membership clubs where they will have conversations about products, services, candidates, and local civic issues. They will share information about the efficacy and value-add of products and services. They will discuss the truthfulness of statements made by product and service providers, the basis of the warnings on the labels, the origin of the product and that country's rules concerning child labor, treatment of women, shipment of weapons to terrorists, the carbon footprint of the vendors, and the after-sale support service, among other things.

The consumers will benefit because (1) they will receive services that are efficiently and truthfully provided; (2) they will buy products that do what they are supposed to do; and (3) prices will fall dramatically because of the reduced need for advertising and because recommender communities will give Procter & Gamble, Johnson & Johnson, and your local law firm the recurring revenue model that they have dreamed about. Yes, among the recipients of pain remedies will be the vendors themselves. Why? Because their cost of search will be greatly reduced.

Creating the Elegant Recommender Community

As the recommender community entrepreneur that I will attempt to train you to become, you will need to learn the singular importance of the words *trust* and *verify*. Members of your community must be individuals who can add value to the community and not be representatives of American Express or Pfizer pretending to be collaborating while promoting their products. When a member of a community of Huntington's disease victims, or their families, speaks of the wonders of a treatment he received with a cocktail of certain drugs or the procedure of a certain hospital, there must be a mechanism for verifying the member's truth. If it is not truth, his membership must be canceled.

You cannot use advertising as a revenue source while operating a recommender community. The early social networks that use advertising as their primary revenue channel—MySpace, Facebook, Bebo, Orkut, and others—are struggling with several inefficiencies. It is important to note that they are oriented toward younger people and, thus, are not role models for disrupting the antelope hunters and capturing their market capitalizations. In fact, these pioneers mistakenly use advertising as their primary source of revenue. That's a no-no. It does not bring efficiencies to the providers of goods and services, and it does not bring efficiencies to consumers. It does the opposite: It wastes money and keeps prices high. Studying MySpace and Facebook will not train you in the gospel of how to create demonstrably viable economic social networks whose task is to solve the pain of high prices, dubious claims, inefficient delivery models, and terrible after-sale support. MySpace and Facebook do not build trust among their members, and the statements of their members are not verified. Wikipedia is the better model, but it, too, is a pioneer with ups and downs in its method of execution. The elegant recommender community, which is the subject of Chapter 1, is member supported; its mission is truthful exchanges of information that benefit the lives of its members; and it will solve the pain of its members.

One of the largest sources of revenues in recommender communities is the anonymized conversations of the members, their product ratings and reviews, and the slicing and dicing of the recommendations and conversations in monthly, quarterly, and annual reports sold to the producers of goods and services that need the data. I present you with 17 other revenue channels in Chapter 1, plus a business model of a very elegant recommender community that you are free to launch. I have another 500 in my head.

Perfect business models are always built on truthfulness. The more that truth flows between buyer and seller, the more perfect is the business model, the greater the trust, the loyalty, and the respect that grows between buyer and seller, and the more efficient is the marketplace. *Efficient* doesn't mean "fair." Taxes are used to redistribute wealth, thus making a market more fair, but less efficient. When economists say a market is "efficient," they mean there is a way to make some players better off while harming somebody else. If Tiger Woods is taxed up to 40 percent of his earnings and his tax payment distributed to the other professional golfers, Tiger is worse off, while the other players benefit.

The youngest person ever to win the Nobel Prize for Economics, Kenneth Arrow, proved that not only are all truthful markets efficient, "all efficient outcomes can be achieved using a competitive market, by adjusting the starting position." Politicians seize on this theorem all the time by taxing success, raising tariffs to support local industries, and granting subsidies to corn farmers (even though they are making a windfall on ethanol). Recommender communities will one day foil politicians who believe that "if it moves, tax it." The recommender social network Rethos.com is on the right track. Advertising is a form of attempting to change the outcome in favor of the advertiser. But, advertising is not to be used in online communities. I will present 17 elegant revenue channels for you to use in Chapter 1, and none of them are advertising based; yet the advertising industry will be reborn as a strategic partner of recommender communities.

Your Recommender Community as Theater

It is a sumptuous impertinence, to quote Cyrano de Bergerac, to launch a social network; but to quote Shakespeare, a successful launch is more honored in the breach than in the observance. The goal of entrepreneurship is to make one's enterprise a substitute for all others in the marketplace while making theirs no substitute for one's own. In so doing, the entrepreneur will disrupt existing businesses while solving the pain of many and creating wealth for himself and the company's early investors.

Think of yourself as an actor facing an audience of the most circumspect and negative critics—picture the food critic, Anton Ego, in the movie *Ratatouille*—and your task on opening night is to save the play and the theater, not merely to win a rave review. The gravitas of the moment, the continual, evolving drama that is the launch of your performance as the lead actor in the play entitled *My Pain-Solving Social Network*, must be imagined and featured as the most important thing you have ever done in your life. The rough, raw conditions of the start-up emphasize the primacy of the entrepreneur as actor—of the dramatic word made fresh by the living actors in an atmosphere of the highest communicative intensity. "Anything inessential in the writing and acting (not to mention set design, which has to be minimal) will not survive the extreme temperatures of this crucible," to quote Harry Eyres, the *Financial Times* columnist. The recommender online community entrepreneur should probably have a background in theater and summer job experience in acting, door-to-door sales, or evangelical preaching; or if that isn't possible, she needs to borrow those competences.

The winning online community entrepreneur will learn more from the styles of the great entrepreneurs of the 1960s—Ray Kroc, Kemmons Wilson, Debbie Fields, and Jean Neditch—than from the geek and geekette entrepreneurs of the Internet era. The peculiar greatness of recommender community entrepreneurs, of whom the readers of this book will someday soon, I trust, compose the majority, and the sense of the sublimity of the occasion stems from a delight in being alive at the right time and in control of events at a critical moment in history. You thrive on the instability of things.

The infinite possibilities of the unpredictable future offer endless opportunities for spontaneous moment-to-moment improvisation and for your large, imaginative, bold strokes that cause important events that change the course of history. It is your time. It is your moment. The floodlights are on you. Treat your recommender community as the theater it is: filled with your script, your clear, brightly colored vision of—and passionate faith in—your views. There will be attempts by big corporations to crush your start-up. Stand firm. You may be sued. So what? Be joyful that you have ruffled big industry's feathers. Put this sign on your white board: *illegitimati non carborundum est*. And believe it. To quote your personal economic advisor, Joseph Schumpeter, "Corporatism may soften creative destruction but will certainly not bring it to a halt." You will read more about the need to be theatrical in launching and executing the business models of recommender communities in Chapter 2.

Mimic the Bakers and Copy Starbucks

An understanding of the concept of scarcity and its opposite, non-scarcity, is vital to your success as a recommender social network entrepreneur. We pay a premium for scarce resources. Tune into the *Antiques Road Show* on PBS and you will see quilts and one-of-a-kind chairs valued at $25,000. An orchestra seat at the Santa Fe Opera goes for $150. A limited-edition Lamborghini sells for $160,000, and you will not have a wide choice of colors to select from.

Then there is the Internet. It is nonscarce resource. And its cousin, the wireless network, is so inexpensive that it, too, is a nonscarce resource. They are both ubiquitous. How then does one make a nonscarce resource scarce? How, then, does one convince other people to pay a price that will result in a profit to the owner of an online community, if every Tom, Dick, and Harry can offer the same thing by registering a domain name and having an online community builder such as OneSite put up a web portal? To put a fine point on it, how does one bring paying customers to the non-scarce web portal that you call your recommender community? And then, how does one bring in the second, the third, the fourth, and so on customers to your new, nonscarce social network?

Have you eaten a pastry lately? Have you bought a coffee at Starbucks recently? The anonymous baker and Howard Schultz, the founder of Starbucks, pulled it off brilliantly. Wheat is grown ubiquitously. Coffee is sold everywhere from Walgreens to Shell stations to restaurants to coffee shops. Wheat and coffee are non-scarce resources. So, how do companies such as Harlan Bakeries and Starbucks do so well? I will explain in Chapter 3, "Mimic the Bakers and Copy Starbucks."

Why Not Start Five Simultaneously?

If you can launch one recommender community and execute its business model elegantly, you can do four or five at the same time. Or you can launch and execute one recommender community and purchase several others that have built non-revenue-producing memberships of 25,000 or more needy souls, but that are lacking a sustainable revenue model and are thus facing foreclosure and extinction. To find struggling communities with which you have familiarity is not difficult. The bed sheets have been pulled up by the sleuthing skills of web services such as compete.com. Losers can't hide anymore. Place a classified ad on Craigslist, or contact all of the venture capital and angel capital funds, and let them know that you will buy some of their disasters. You will not have to use much cash to make a purchase. Just issue a security, such as your company's common stock, that will enable the venture capitalists and the angels to avoid a writedown, as writedowns are counted as 100 percent deductions against their 20 percent participations in winners. They will be able to avoid a writedown if they can persuade their auditors that the stock that you gave them has value. It may or it may not, but that's how the game is played. There are thousands of well-funded social networks that have failed to gain traction. You can pick and choose the ones you want. You will be able to buy them inexpensively and fix their business models, by introducing some of the revenue channels in Chapter 1.

Markus Frind, a 29-year-old Vancouver, BC, entrepreneur, launched the online dating source, plentyoffish.com, which operates almost entirely on autopilot. Now five years old, plentyoffish.com earns Markus about $10 million a year, and Markus devotes fewer than 10 hours a week to running it. The members do all of the work, providing dating advice to each other. There are 1.4 million active users, and revenues come largely from recommending books and other dating sites that kick back recommender fees. And plentyoffish is not the owner's full-time occupation. I call this pure elegance of execution.

Craigslist also runs almost entirely on autopilot. It charges employees for job listings in 10 of its 450 cities, and charges brokers for apartment listings. All other listings are free.

Craigslist has an Alexa rank of 63 while plentyoffish.com sits at 788, both near the top.

In Chapter 4, I ask the question: "Why not start five simultaneously?" I will explain why it might be the right thing for you to do.

Loyalty and Passion Builders

Having the good fortune of being born and raised in Knoxville, Tennessee, I have been to my fair share of evangelical tent meetings and creekside Pentecostal church services. I have seen the passion of the true believers, and I have heard the bacchanalian screams and orgiastic yelps of those who speak in tongues when the Holy Spirit enters their bodies. The cadence and delivery of the evangelical preachers and the sing-song, almost lyrical delivery of the African-American ministers in the South have not been lost on the founders of insurance companies and multilevel marketing companies. The heads of any association, church, or marketing organization must grow membership and hold their interest, while arousing them to seed the flock—bring in more members. These organizations borrow styles from one another. For those who do it well, like the Reverend Billy Graham and the late great Mary Kay Ash, the passion in the room is palpable. Ms. Ash, who founded Mary Kay Cosmetics, sold to women through the party-plan marketing channel. She preached to her 5,000 independent beauty consultants, "I built this company for you. If you are here today, you're too smart to go home and scrub floors. You are spending one dollar time on a one penny chore." Most of her sales staff hire housekeepers within a few months of signing on with Mary Kay. You can feel the passion in the air at any of these tent meetings, or multilevel marketing company sales conferences.

It is rarely seen in online communities—this evangelical intensity set aflame by inspired preachers and their numinous minions. And it needs to be, in order to create online communities of enormous value to their members as well as monetary value to their founders. I have seen it done offline numbers of times, and I will show you how to bring these offline passion-building tools to your online community.

Disruption: The Sumptuous Impertinence

MySpace and Facebook are the established market-dominant icons in the field of generalized social networks. Give them credit for building online communities that serve broad social needs. The next great wave of online communities will focus on specific interests such as health, travel, improvement of government services, wealth, beauty, neighborhood watches, hobbies, protecting one's estate, and rating the abilities and prices of lawyers, realtors, electricians, hospitals, physicians, judges, school teachers, and vendors of a host of products and services for the home. Thousands of online communities with sharper focuses than we have yet seen in any socioeconomic marketplace will be formed to nucleate people who feel compelled to join—indeed, thankful for the opportunity to join and collaborate about a topic of great import to them—and to bring truth, their truth, to the community of truth-seekers and petitioners that will inevitably weed out inadequate products and services and recommend and support the best. The result will yield more competition and lower prices, which will massively disrupt many established industries and transfer the wealth that their stakeholders once enjoyed to the stakeholders in online communities.

So truthful and effective will the best-of-breed recommender communities become, that the marketplace of products and services will pay them to brand, make changes to, suggest prices for, and launch new products and services.

We will ask the question, but leave it to you, the reader, to answer: Should the members share in the wealth that the founders of online communities create? When AOL bought BEBO for $850 million in April 2008, a number of BEBO members sued AOL for some of the purchase price, claiming that the members created most of the value—most of the $850 million. They are right, of course. Or are they? Although the suit didn't go anywhere, perhaps it should have.

Should members of communities be offered stock ownership in the community owner? Home Depot gives 100 shares of its stock to new employees. Not very much, but a nice gesture. We will kick this question around in Chapter 6.

It is an important topic for discussion. The shift in wealth will be in the trillions of dollars. Take the cost of search of all consumer products and services companies—that is, their advertising and marketing dollars—and transfer it to the market values of all social networks engaged in review, rate, and recommend services, and divide that by 500 successful recommender communities and you get a number in the $10 billion range for each of the 500 winning companies. As they say in New York, "Dat ain't chopped liver."

Maximize Your Selling Price

Are you having too much fun? Or should you sell? If you choose the latter route, in Chapter 7, I will explain how to sell at the top.

Irritation is a business strategy. We know, because the print media that follows the emergence of online communities tells us so—that consumer-oriented businesses hear the footsteps of recommender social networks coming toward them in greater and greater numbers; but they are frightened and irritated by their loss of muscle and their seeming inability to mount a defense. Unilever's head of digital media strategy, Kevin George, told *Strategy & Business* reporters Andrea Rasmussen and Carolyn Ude, "First, we have changed our corporate venture to one that encourages taking risks. Second, we've done a great job of focusing on how to adapt and use digital media in marketing." I am doubtful about either statement. Unilever spent $848 million, the third-most of all consumer advertisers in the world in 2006, on "alternative media," according to *New York Times* reporter Louise Story, in her article, "The New Advertising Outlet: Your Life," October 20, 2007. And although I am not aware of Unilever's digital media marketing strategy, this

I know to be true: *Placing ads on Facebook, MySpace, and Second Life are worthless tactics to find new customers.*

Unilever and its ilk are irritated. Because their senior marketing managers are uncomfortable and squirming in their seats as they see themselves standing in the unemployment lines in a few months, they will act carelessly. They may offer to acquire your recommender community. Or like Microsoft, which invested $240 million to buy 1.6 percent of Facebook—an unwise move, in my opinion, as Facebook is not a truthful social network in the economic, not the moral, sense of the word—they might offer to buy a piece of your social network for an unrealistically high valuation. Encourage it. The current going price for the purchase of social networks is 20 times trailing twelve-month revenues. The transfer of wealth into your pocket from a great commercial enterprise, whose managers you have scared into weeping into their linen pillows, is always encouraged.

This is your time to create great wealth. If you want to do it, I will show you how in Chapter 7.

Wrap-Up

Finally, I have saved perhaps the best for last. In Chapter 8, "Wrap-Up," I discuss your potentially enormous value to our planet.

I mean this in a heroic sense. Isaiah Berlin, in his epic biography of Winston Churchill, wrote that the peculiar quality of greatness and a sense of the sublimity of the occasion stems from a delight in being alive at "the right time" and in control of events at a critical moment in history. This strength will enhance your energy and drive, as it did Winston Churchill's in the Battle of Britain, when he said: "It is impossible to quell the inward excitement which comes from a prolonged balancing of terrible things." Which new, large, central human issues will your recommender social network solve? Truthfulness in the sale of goods and services? Lowering the price of goods and services? Enabling local collective social action to improve government services and undertake collaborative community improvement projects, such as restoring blighted sections of our nation's cities and towns? The introduction of more efficient business models in the sale of goods and services? Improved product distribution systems that reduce the number of vehicles on the highways? Carbon footprint minimization criteria in every management decision? Sharing medical information among families of patients with terminal illness to extend their lives? Effectively building sustainable recommender social networks will make you a legitimate hero.

Frog Boiling

The multibillion-dollar question over the next few years is this: Will the antelope hunters—the consumer products and service industries, sometimes referred to as the "brands"—continue to control their customers through advertising, shelf-space management, couponing, catalogues, and web site retailing, or will recommender communities utilizing the wisdom of crowds to vote on the best products and services actually instruct the vast number of consumers on which product or service to purchase?

If the entrepreneurs who build the recommender communities execute their business models with elegance and efficiency—and I will provide the best instructions for doing so—then the recommender communities will creatively disrupt the antelope hunters.

The reason is not that difficult to see: The antelope hunt business model is too inefficient and has too many moving parts to operate effectively; and the advertising messages are not truthful in an age when online communities can be formed, paid for, and maintained by consumers who enjoy collaborating with others, who are energized and impelled to seek out others with whom to exchange ideas, and who love the search and shared functionality made possible by the Internet.

But the senior managements of the antelope hunt companies, with their bloated marketing staffs and sales forces that support their tedious and expensive business model, are like frogs swimming in water that becomes increasingly hotter. Marc Ventresca, a lecturer at Said Business School at Oxford, wrote, "Adaptation can sometimes be dangerous, but the hazard isn't apparent until it is too late. The managers who are aware of disruptive innovation, but who put off responding to it are like frogs swimming around in water where the temperature is gradually rising. The steadily rising heat is no cause for alarm until the water is so hot that death is imminent."

Entrepreneurs of the world, unite. If you want to accompany me to a frog boil, read on. Send me your recommender social network, smart start-up ideas to dsilver@sfcapital.com. A revolution is coming in the way goods and services are sold to consumers. The mighty brands and their service providers will be disrupted with a massive, multitrillion-dollar wealth transfer, with the plums— valuable stock certificates—FedExed to the owners, managers, and perhaps members of recommender social networks. Consumers' pain will be solved by collaborating to obtain lower prices, better products, and improved services. The "brands" will become reliant on the communities for their launch of new products and to attract customers. Control of many social, civic, commercial, and cultural decisions will pass from the providers to the communities. The shift will be the most important change in socioeconomics since the invention of bread.

Hang onto your forks. We're going to a frog boil.

1

Eighteen Sustainable Revenue Channels

As THE GREAT ONE, WAYNE GRETZKY, once said, "Always be skating to where you think the puck is going to land." The same applies to building a business from the ground up. When sketching out a business model for any business you might be thinking about starting, always picture the most desirable end result. For example, in the case of recommender communities, your most desirable end result is users group meetings. These are known by their modern name, *industry trade shows*. They are huge moneymakers because their producers rent air inexpensively for a few days, and sublet it at very high prices. The air is space in a hotel for seminars, exhibitor space, reprints of seminar topics, souvenirs, and space for attendees, who pay entrance fees, to meet with other users, speak with exhibitors, and listen to and query speakers at the seminars.

If your recommender community attracts 5,000 members to its users group meeting, each of whom pays $300 to attend, and 50 corporate exhibitors, each of which pays $40,000 for their booths, and if you take a 10 percent slice of $200 per night for the hotel rooms, then before other revenue items, your users group meeting will generate $1.5 million in attendee fees, $2 million in exhibitor space revenue, $500,000 in sponsor fees, and $200,000 in a slice of the room rates, for a gross revenue of $4.2 million. Your costs will be less than $500,000. As the number of attendees grows over the years, all of your other revenue channels grow as well, but not your costs. To paraphrase Irving Berlin, "There's no business like the trade show business." Ask Sheldon Adelson, who sold Comdex for $2 billion.

The loyalty and camaraderie that the users group meeting will generate will embolden the members when they return to their homes and click on for more reviewing, ranking, and rating of their products and services categories. And the theater and evangelizing that can be accomplished at users group meetings can create the glue that keeps your recommender community growing and glowing. We will talk about time-tested theatrical techniques to build passion for the community in Chapter 2.

With that endgame in mind, let's turn our attention to the more propinquitous revenue channels to select—from the date of the launch forward. After all, it is near-term revenue that you are interested in, to make sure cash flow keeps coming in and outside venture capital is minimized. As James Bond said to Pussy Galore as he pulled her closer, "Nothing propinks like propinquity." And so it is with launching an online community: near-term cash flow. Thus, in reviewing the 18 revenue channels, select the ones for your community that bring in the cash the fastest.

I didn't just stumble onto these 18 revenue channels; I came up with them out of necessity. As an angel investor in online communities and mobile social networks (see my company's portfolio at www.sfcapital.com), my angel group frequently invests $300,000 to $500,000 of a community's start-up capital. Our angel group receives, let's say, 20 percent ownership, and the entrepreneurial team keeps 80 percent.

It is my task to avoid a follow-on round of venture capital, because if that happens, our angel group will be diluted to around

10 percent, and the entrepreneurial team will have its stake desiccated to around 40 percent before stock options. At the time of exit, for—pick a figure—$50 million, my personal 2 percent interest gets diluted down to 1 percent or $500,000 from $1 million. Not pleasant. In order to prevent dilution of this magnitude, I observed and conceived of a number of new revenue channels to quickly bring cash into online communities. That kind of defensive thinking also led me to flush out the mechanics of the review, rank, and recommend functions of online communities, which, as you know if you've come this far, is my favorite online community pain-solving modality.

Lets go into depth on each of the revenue channels, and then create a business model for a recommender community that shows in which month the cash comes in from each channel along with an explanation that persuades the payor to pay.

Subscription Fees

There is a price sensitivity about paying for services on the Internet, because it is itself a nonscarce resource. Accordingly, although your members may be able to pay a monthly fee, they may not be willing to pay. Monthly subscription fees can be charged after a year of operations and after the members see and believe that their membership has value—that they are getting value for their money. The amount of the monthly fee depends not only on the clout that your recommender community delivers, but on the topic it covers. A higher fee can be charged by health and financial services communities, because they are of huge concern to the people who are most likely to join them; that is, older people who want to maximize their retirement accounts and live longer, healthier lives. Beauty, sex, dating, legal services, and buying a home are worth quite a bit as well, but not as much as health and wealth. Fighting crime, cleaning up a community, electing honest politicians, eliminating title insurance, encouraging oil companies to invest in alternative energy, and making credit reports more accurate are probably worth a little less.

A graduate student in economics scratching her head to find a good topic for a Ph.D. thesis could do a better job of ranking the pain level of people issue by issue and country by country than I can. An examination of the gross profit margins of publicly held companies by industry provides considerable insight. The higher the gross profit margin, the more confused and murky the solution that the company is delivering. Certain industries have very few competitors, and thus have monopoly power, and that is the case with "embarrassment products" such as tampons and condoms, where it is very difficult to explain in print or television ads why product B is superior to product A. Or take the case of Fair Isaac Company, which has persuaded the credit rating agencies of the accuracy of their algorithms. Fair Isaac sports a gross profit margin of 63.3 percent, and credit rating agency Equifax Corp's is 59.3 percent—both high by anyone's ranking system. Other publicly held companies with exceptionally high gross profit margins are Johnson & Johnson at 70.9 percent, Merck at 76.6 percent, Novartis at 72.5 percent, Pfizer at 84.1 percent, and Bristol-Myers Squibb at 68.8 percent— all pharmaceutical companies. The correlation between the rapid formation of online communities seeking truthfulness about health care and the high gross profit margin of pharmaceutical companies is readily apparent. If you launch a recommender community in this field, and do it successfully, some of that huge gross profit margin will transfer over to the wealth of your community.

Tip Jar

When a member of your community does an outstanding job of reporting a material transgression by a corporation that, for instance, has been calling its product "green" or "organic" when it isn't, and the report leads to a downgraded recommendation by the votes of the members, the reporter should be rewarded with tips. A tip-jar window on the home page of your community that accepts credit card payments should be set up. Into that window will pour a number of $20 to $100 payments. Remember to set a minimum tip of $20 or so, in order to encourage members to dig deeply and thoroughly in their research, thus making the tips worthwhile. If 5,000 members each send $20 to the reporter, the aggregate payment will be $100,000. Of that amount, the reporter will receive 70 percent and your community 30 percent.

That ratio was set by OhMyNews, a Korean citizens' journalism community that invented the tip jar-method of payment. OhMyNews has an Alexa rating of 53,352 (see www.alexa.com, which ranks the popularity of web sites).

Reputation Management Fee

The members will want a continual flow of information on many factors affecting their community. Their loyalty to the community needs glue. The glue is the newsletter, along with the money they can earn in tip jars and their stock ownership in your community, about which more later. One of the main news items is naming or "outing" the corporations or enterprises that have attempted to place employees in the community who act as ordinary citizen members, but in fact are attempting to spread the biased gospel of their employer's product or service. There will also be defectors who hack into the community solely to throw it off of its mission and distract the members with gobbledygook. These perpetrators can be named in the community's weekly newsletter in a column entitled "Red Brigade." By reading the column, members will be warned not to share information with subversives. In the late 1940s and into the 1950s, the New York City Police Department formed the Red Squad, which was made up of police officers who searched for communists. The title was later changed several times to fit the mood of the city. It was named the Radical Squad for a while and then, for some reason, Public Relations.

If you choose "Red Brigade," and every other community founder chooses the same name, then an alert and prescient entrepreneur can launch redbrigade.com to gather the names of all defectors in all social networks and provide a useful service that all community owners will gladly pay for.

The point of the Red Brigade is to maintain the truthfulness of the conversations between members in your community. If someone pierces your community's mission as a place where concerned citizens can discuss their experiences with financial advisors (actually, salespersons) from the life insurance and annuity industry, and this intruder then makes sales pitches for Hartford Financial Group, she could destroy everything you are trying to build. Wikipedia has had a few instances of contributors spreading gross lies, and its "truth squad" had to be quickly assembled to vet the truthfulness of submissions. This could happen in your community; in fact, plan for it and make certain you admit people of the highest probity and rectitude.

There are several ways to investigate the backgrounds of both the Red Brigade truth squad members and new members who appear to be overtly pushing the products and services of a corporation as well as defectors and turnstile jumpers who join the community to disrupt it. One site is www.whois.sc, which will tell you the ownership of a web site. So, if I join your community with the e-mail address dsilver@excrutiatinglyupset.com, you can Google www.whois.sc and learn who owns the URL. This valuable repository does not charge for searches. Another site is www.backgroundspi.com, which does charge for searches. It will tell you if a person has a felony record.

The newsletter needs to contain more information for its members than just the reports of the Red Brigade. The members will want to know if their efforts are resulting in any changes to the industry or the governmental agency that they are trying to disrupt in order to improve its efficiencies. The members will want to know membership growth figures, average daily user figures, the community's Alexa rating, whether any major media have reported on its achievements, means by which they may purchase stock in the community, and what the stock price is worth week by week. The newsletter should also report outstanding pieces of research and the tip-jar value of the reports as well as newsworthy stories about the industry or the governmental agency being disrupted and made more efficient.

The newsletter is a scarce resource within the community, and it is worth charging an admission price for it. If a member wants to enter and read the newsletter page on the community's web site, that is worth something. Five dollars a month, or $60 a year, is a reasonable fee. If you finish your first year with 25,000 members, and if 20,000 of them pay the monthly fee upfront, and get a $10 discount, your company will have earned $1 million. That is a lot of float for a start-up company, and it will obviate raising $1 million of venture capital and giving up some precious stock ownership.

Slice and Dice the Conversation

This revenue channel requires you to make the e-mail addresses of the members anonymous and ambiguous, using some technical services, which are doubtless purchasable online. The e-mail addresses need to be changed continually so that the member is never identified. If their pseudonymous e-mail names are not made anonymous, your community could die before it has much of a chance to live. Be paranoid about the critical aspect of executing your business model, because your competitors will be all over you like white on rice, not to mention the damaged member who will likely be irate.

Various departments of the companies or governmental agencies that members of your community will be talking about as well as rating and ranking will be extremely curious about the conversations that take place in your community. "Curiosity" is probably an understatement. A better phrase is "seriously concerned," because the people who want to know how their product and service is being discussed, ranked, and rated by the wisdom of crowds could have their jobs on the line.

Brett Hurt, CEO of BazaarVoice.com, which manages Wal-Mart's online community said, "Wal-Mart is particularly interested in the negative reviews of members, such as which boom box cover scratches the most, and they react quickly to correct the problem they hear about."

Let's say that your recommender community is designed to rate and rank the credit rating process from credit card issuing companies, to the rating agencies that gather data from them, to Fair Isaac Corp, which gathers the data from the rating agencies and compiles the FICO scores of millions of Americans. The community is formed, and the members contribute their stories of the speed at which the credit card companies issue a 30-days-late or a 60-days-late report to the credit rating agencies. Let's say that the credit card—issuing companies are named Ajax, Bozo, Chumbly, Darth, and Ebo. The members report that Ajax always calls first, as soon as the member is 10 days past 30 days late, and asks for a payment and warns the cardholder that she will be reported only if she becomes 60 days late. They report that Bozo calls only 20 percent of its cardholders and reports the delinquent cardholders for being 30 days late if they become 45 days late. The members report that Chumbly calls 10 percent of its 30-days-delinquent cardholders and asks for a payment, and warns the 10 percent that they will be reported for being 30 days late if they go 40 days late. The members report that Darth does not call at all, but only reports cardholders who are 60 days late. And the members report that Ebo does not call at all and reports cardholders who are 30 days late. Ebo is going to see a sudden rash of customer flight.

One 30-day-late report to the credit reporting agencies results in a FICO score of 770 dropping to 735. For the cardholder who seeks to borrow $500,000 to buy a house, a decline in a FICO score of 5 percent could mean that the borrower will pay 1 percent more in interest, which in this example is $150,000 over 30 years.

The members rank the credit card issuing companies. Ajax gets 90 percent approval from the members; three-fourths of the members report that they are going to tear up their Ebo cards and two-thirds of the members say they are going to cut their Darth cards in half. Bozo and Chumbly cardholders say they plan to work their balances down to $100 and refrain from using the cards.

The conversations that lead up to the rankings of the card issuers can be sliced and diced into reports that can be sold to the banks and card-issuing companies for $100,000 apiece, or your community can offer Ebo a special deal: for instance, "We won't report the results of our members' ranking of Ebo against its competitors for a special price of $10 million." The $10 million can be distributed 70/30 among the members, with the members receiving the larger slice. *Ah*, oligopsony power at its finest. Call it hush money, but Ebo has the staff to have held focus groups, and it didn't. Now it must pay because the wisdom of crowds has spoken. The price charged Darth could be as high as the one charged Ebo, and for the same reasons. *Ah*, the wisdom of Willy Loman's wife: "Attention must be paid."

Port the Community to Mobile Phones

Mobile social networks have a distinct advantage over online communities: When people send voice messages, text messages, or documents from one mobile phone or personal digital assistant (PDA) to another, they are charged by the carrier for the minutes of connect time, and the receiving mobile phone user is charged 10 cents per message. Your community will be generating content, and the minutes that are earned by Verizon, AT&T Mobile, Sprint, T-Mobile, or Bell Canada, or any other mobile carrier, are the reason the call was made. Thus, the mobile carriers are willing to share some of their minute charges with the owners of content. Of course, you have to get your community's content onto the decks of the wireless carriers, and that means negotiating directly with the carriers or going through an aggregator such as Wireless Developer Agency, Lansing, MI, which is under contract to a number of the wireless carriers to select the best content to go onto their decks. Games are very popular and they are typically selected to fill the top positions on the decks. Recommender social networks will soon replace games because of their enormous value-add.

This change will occur for several rational reasons. As the population of web users ages, the people spending more and more time on the Web begin spending less time on games and more time on serious issues; so time is in your favor. Second, the published ratings, rankings, and recommendations of your community could be interesting content that members are likely to want to share with a friend as she walks into a Toyota dealership to see what the automobile recommender community thinks about the new Camry, or to share with a friend who is about to select a law firm to represent her in a contract dispute to see what the attorney recommender community thinks about the law firms in her town.

By sending out ratings, rankings, and surveys to nonmembers—an activity that you should encourage—you are broadening your outreach to new members, and the cost of bringing in new members is borne by current members.

In the near future, RFID chips will be embedded in consumer products, and they will transmit information gathered by the recommender communities and distributed to the vendors to be transferred into the transmitter chip. A consumer with a mobile phone that acts as a receiver for the RFID transmitter chip will be able to read the ratings, rankings, and recommendations right off the packages and not have to request the information from a member of the community that gathers the data on that particular line of products. When the RFID chip revolution comes around, the strongest recommender communities will be able to force the vendors to embed the ratings, rankings, and recommendations of their members onto their packages. They won't have a choice, if the oligopsony power of the successful recommender communities becomes as enormous as I believe it will. (By the way, I know about the RFID chip because the first iteration of it on the consumer level, the EZ Pass, was discovered at the Venture Capital Club of New Mexico, and the inventor, Gary Seawright, a Los Alamos, NM pharmacologist, raised some of his angel capital at the club.)

The revenue channel in the form of payments from mobile phone companies could become significant—but perhaps, not for a year or 18 months. Your community needs to gain traction first and foremost. But, when you are ready to sit down with the carriers and negotiate a slice of the pie, you can expect to receive around 50 percent of the charges they earn on the minutes used to carry your community's content. Payments are made every 90 days like clockwork, and because they are so regular, accounts receivable financing can be raised from specialty lenders who like telecom receivables, and you can borrow on the future payments and thus avoid taking in venture capital. A typical advance rate on telecom accounts receivable is 85 percent, and the interest rate you are likely to pay is in the range of prime plus 1 to prime plus 2 percent. And if the lenders ask you for your personal guarantee, tell them the meeting is over. I don't believe in them for early-stage, entrepreneurial companies. Use this phrase to negotiate away the personal guarantee request: "All my net worth is tied up in the company, and you know that; so why would you want to hold the same collateral twice—the receivable and my guarantee to pay you if the receivable isn't collected?" It is double dipping, and once again I repeat: Do not give your personal guarantee to a loan backed up by contractual receivables from the nation's wireless carriers. They're good for the money.

Accounts receivable lenders that like telecom receivables are Bridge Bank, Marquette, Capital Source, Capital Temp Funds, and Rosenthal & Rosenthal, among others.

The sale of synthetic currency to your members is an additional revenue channel. To get there, you will need to grow your membership to somewhere around SecondLife's size. They have close to 8 million members and 1.5 million average daily users. SecondLife has an Alexa ranking of 2,957, way up there.

Kudos

This revenue channel is similar to the tip jar but also borrows on the notion of the "unexpected reward." People love to be acknowledged, and when a member performs a certain act of brilliance that benefits all of the other members, she can be rewarded by the community management with a bag of synthetic currency and the membership can be encouraged to pay her as well. As this isn't real money, and she can spend it only within the community and with designated vendors and retailers, it is limited; but nonetheless, it is physical, it shines like gold coins, and it brings a sense of pride and accomplishment. When I attended one of the earliest meetings of Kentucky Fried Chicken franchisees back in the 1970s, I noticed that the franchisees wore string ties held together with metallic images of the Colonel. For outstanding achievement, the franchisees' Colonel tie-holder was gold. For not-so-outstanding achievement, the franchisees sported silver Colonel tie-holders. And if your franchise had not done so well, you had to hold your tie together with a paper clip or a rubber band.

Insurance companies and mutual fund marketing companies give kudos at their annual national and regional meetings. For outstanding sales in the Pacific Northwest Region, for instance, the winner is announced and he trots up to the brightly lit podium through a wall of high-fiving hands and shouts to receive an engraved pen set and the embrace of the head of sales and his blonde assistant. Multilevel marketing companies use kudos as a form of reward for outstanding sales. Mary Kay Cosmetics uses pink Cadillacs.

My point of differentiation is to have the community members do some of the rewarding. It's more meaningful, and they have to buy the synthetic currency from the community owner, which means you pick up another revenue channel.

Users Group Meetings

The ultimate goal of your recommender community is the annual users group meeting. Any member can come, as long as he pays for his air fare, his room and board, and an admission fee. Your money will come from selling exhibitor booths. I don't recommend your permitting booth rental to the companies whose products and services your community rates, ranks, and recommends. But there is a whole host of manufacturers and services providers who want to meet your members. The largest group of potential exhibitor booth renters is the computer and software industry, closely followed by the telecom industry, the travel industry (eco travel), food, media, publishing (relevant books), and furniture (media centers for the home). You will see in the business models that follow how to set up and run a successful users group meeting with a highly positive cash flow.

You may have noticed that my orbital summary of the revenue channels in their evection through all possible galaxies of cash flow did not include affiliate ad networks, advertorials, setting up a not-for-profit, team building products, facilities management, or branding fees. I haven't forgotten these stars and planets. They are quite novel and little used, but they may become the most important revenue channels that you will use in solving the pain that consumer products and service producers are feeling as TV viewership declines and web usership and online purchasing rises. Exhibit 1.1 shows the magnitude of the pain that your online community may heal.

As the population of TV viewers ages, and this applies to print media and radio as well, consumer brand advertisers must reach out to web users and online purchasers. Alas, the latter group, raised on the fundamental belief that the Internet is free, click through the ads for the most part. The dilemma for consumer brand advertisers is to find a way to reach web users and online purchasers to present their messages and to introduce new brands in a manner that produces documentable sales. Recommender online communities can achieve that for them. Recommender online communities can heal that pain. Here are some of the newest revenue channels cocooning in the business plan drafts of entrepreneurs.

Sponsorships: All of us have seen the "powered by . . ." sponsorships on the home pages of many web sites. For instance, CNNMoney.com is "powered by . . ." Cisco. The sponsor has paid for the right to have its name front and center on the home page

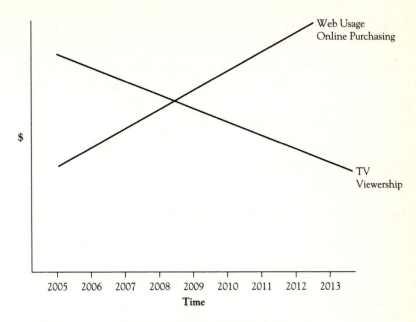

Web Usage
Online Purchasing

TV
Viewership

$

2005 2006 2007 2008 2009 2010 2011 2012 2013

Time

EXHIBIT 1.1   The Pain-Healing Opportunity

of CNNMoney.com, a popular business and financial news web portal. When you launch your recommender social network, call on some corporate giants whose products are not going to be the subject of reviews and ratings in your community, and sell them "powered by . . ." links on your home page. Share your business plan with them, and make sure they understand that at times your members may be outspoken about issues that concern them, and that this could mean speaking negatively about industry companies or government agencies. Several politically agnostic candidates for sponsorships are makers of computer equipment, chips, software, mobile phones, cabling, printers, printer cartridges, and other stuff that enables the Internet to operate. Intel Corp., American Micro Devices, Cisco Systems, Hewlett-Packard, IBM, Epson, and Dell come immediately to mind. Charge them as much as the market will bear, and explain that you plan to port your community to mobile phones and to television, and each time it is ported, the names on the home page that power the community will be seen by many more viewers than just those who have joined the community. If you can collect $60,000 a year per "powered by . . ." slot that you sell, that is a terrific accomplishment for a start-up. Take the money and say thank you. You've just sold something to support a community that hasn't even launched.

The J.D. Powers Business Model

This business model is known as the "validation business," and *wow!* Is it ever a barn burner. There are very few companies in the business of giving out awards to companies for being the best at this or that, and so the barriers to entry are low. J.D. Powers owns and operates call centers, where young people call consumers and ask their opinions of cars, trucks, and other consumer products. J.D. Powers charges the members of the industries it surveys. Oprah Winfrey has validation power and can do wonders for novels. She flew out to Santa Fe in 2007 with her camera crew to interview the publicity-shy Cormac McCarthy, who would not go to Chicago, to discuss his terrific novel, *The Road*. Ms. Winfrey spent a morning with Mr. McCarthy at the Santa Fe Institute, a think tank that studies chaos theory in its many forms, from race relations to getting tenants out of a 50-story building when a fire is reported on one of the floors and there are only four exit doors. In typical Winfrey style, she stayed for lunch and listened to the latest in chaos theory and presented the Institute with a Winfrey-size check. Another validator is *Good Housekeeping* magazine, with its well-known "Seal of Approval."

A recommender community would find it difficult to compete with Oprah Winfrey in the book rating and recommending field, because she is a beloved public figure. But, all of the other marketplaces are available—financial services, legal services, communications, regional offices of the Internal Revenue Service, computers, insurance and annuities, colleges and graduate schools, credit card companies, commercial banks, pharmaceutical companies, regulatory agencies, and the like. And your recommender community will be able to generate its data from raw data: that is, the actual words of the members of the community. J.D. Powers doesn't collect data that way. Its call center personnel write down what they hear, and there can be errors in transmission. Angieslist.com, yelp.com, cityvoter.com, and others are well on their way to becoming great recommender communities in some of these markets.

Who is the payor for validating information? Members of the industry being studied. It's a little like the *Who's Who in America* business, the so-called *vanity business*. You can get your name in *Who's Who in America*, but if you're not a celebrity, you have to pay for the insertion. The validation business works the same way. You take a couple of people with strong voices and good scripts and put them on the phone to the CEOs of the companies your recommender community studies. Your people ask the CEOs if they would like to see a report on how their such-and-such products were rated against the competition, with a million voters (or however many members you have at the time). They may resist at first; but, then you tell them that the ratings and rankings report will be sent to CNN, Bloomberg, MSNBC, the *Wall Street Journal*, the *New York Times*, the *Financial Times* . . . and by then they have gotten out their checkbooks.

Synthetic Currency

I am all about synthetic currencies for recommender communities. I believe it is a differentiator and adds something of a design feature to the process of persuading large corporations and governmental agencies to do the right thing. We know they can do things right, but they need to be persuaded to do the right thing, to borrow Peter Drucker's definition of judgment. The community members should vote on what these judgment calls should be. But some are obvious. Many consumer products companies trade with countries whose judicial systems are oppressive to women. These countries may be banned by the federal government, but the corporations trans-ship to them anyhow through Qatar or Bahrain.

Many manufacturers of consumer products make components for their products in coal-fired plants, and we know that coal is a major carbon emitter. Many consumer products are shipped to warehouses via trucks that burn regular rather than biodiesel fuels. There are various software programs that reduce the number of truck deliveries, hence carbon footprints, such as pallet optimizers and load balancers, sold by Cape Systems and others, but very few vendors use them. Pharmaceutical companies with their 70 and 80 percent gross profit margins could take a 1 percent hit to their margins by dropping the price of drugs that could be distributed by the Gates Foundation and other NGOs to sick people in poverty-stricken countries in Africa.

The synthetic currency can be awarded by the community in the form of kudos to its members to form committees within the community to work on these projects. Or, as is done at SecondLife, which sells Linden Dollars to its members for trading within the community for land purchases, and used in multiplayer games to purchase higher status and weapons, your community can sell synthetic currency to its members, which can then be recommended to the vendors in the industry in which the community is focused as a form of payment for their products. How about the "carbon footprint reducer" kudos, or "carbfoot" dollars spendable on Johnson & Johnson products sold at Walgreens, if Johnson & Johnson energetically agrees to pallet optimize and load balance? A web application company will have to be launched to act as a currency exchange for your community's currency and the synthetic currency of other communities. And the story gets better. If retailers carry the products sold to them by vendors in the industry your community studies, you can recommend that the retailers accept payment in your community's synthetic currency. There is currently an online currency exchange company, called IGE, which exchanges synthetic for real currency; but, clearly others need to be formed to handle the increased volume. Allcom Corp. is creating an online currency exchange company. You can do it in house, and earn the spread. Operating a currency exchange business within your social network is yet another revenue channel.

Affiliate Ad Networks

This revenue channel requires that you build your online community to run on the Web and be concomitantly portable to television. On the six o'clock evening news, and again at ten o'clock, for many of the nation's local TV stations, there is not enough news, and a three- to five-minute story tucked in between sports and weather would delight the producers. The idea isn't new. These stories are called "infomercials" or "advertorials." These are stories that are produced to look like news, but in fact are informative stories about something that could be of interest to the viewers, such as a visit to a vineyard. For certain kinds of social networks, what's going on in the conversations of the members could easily take up five minutes and provide wonderful stories for the viewers.

If your community is one that was organized to bring back the Ozzie-and-Harriet neighborhoods of 1950s, as is Groundswellmedia. com, a Los Angeles, CA, social network, replete with efforts to encourage volunteerism, clean up vacant lots so children can play there safely, discourage rampant development of strip centers, paint crosswalks, and cooperate in other efforts, the get-togethers can be videoed and uploaded into TV infomercials.

Suppose your community gathers the carbon footprint reductions (and increases) of America's major industrial companies and creates a scoring system such as the Dow Jones Industrial Average for stocks. The conversations of the members who gather the data can make an interesting infomercial.

Who pays and who gets paid? The "powered by . . ." sponsors pay the TV stations, since their logos will be on the screen for the full five minutes. For video ads, the going CPM, or cost per thousand sets of eyeballs tuned to the station, is $30 to $70. If the local TV station in Sacramento has 600,000 viewers for its six o'clock news, the sponsors would pay $18,000, from which the community would slice off a 15 percent advertising agency fee, or $2,700. If the community has six sponsors, and all six want to have their logo seen by Sacramentans, the TV station will take in $108,000 less the fee to the community of $16,200.

But one market a business does not make. As Cecil B. DeMille supposedly said when filming the *Life of Christ* in the 1930s, "What do you mean only 12 disciples? I need thousands." The same with infomercials. You will need thousands of local TV stations to turn the Affiliate Ad Network into a serious revenue channel. If your community's story is sold to 100 local TV stations each week for 20 weeks, it will make $3,440,000. And the event can be reproduced quarterly, with new material. Your community will earn 15 percent of that, the typical ad agency fee.

Plus, your community will engage with people who may not have heard of it, and a number of them may join to find out for themselves how much fun your group of collaborators has been having.

A Boon to Local Retailers

Now that you have brought millions of dollars to the local TV station, let's see what you can do for local retailers, and this means newspapers and magazines as well. Let's call your community seriousgardeners.com, and the nucleating issue of the community is to share information about what soil additives, fertilizers, and plants flourish best under what conditions, what geographies, and with what kind of care. In northern New Mexico, we are plagued by grasshoppers, and most of us who garden would give our eye teeth to learn how to get rid of the leaf chewers.

Seriousgardeners.com reviews, ranks, and recommends soil additives for tomato and lettuce plants, and announces the winning additive. Let's call the winning soil additive "Tomato and Lettuce Growth Helper," and let's name its manufacturer Helen of Soil. The community makes stickers available on its web site called "Approved by" stickers and these can be plucked off by garden supply stores around the country and affixed to every package of Helen of Soil. An invoice then gets mailed to Helen of Soil asking for a redemption fee of 10 cents a package for using seriousgardeners.com's "Approved by" sticker to promote their product. Helen of Soil will have to agree to this program, but why wouldn't they? Their marketing department didn't have to lift a finger; the wisdom of crowds is better than any focus group they could have engaged. Once again, for designing, developing, and implementing the program, the community earns an advertising agency fee of

15 cents, or a penny and a half per package. If a million packages bear the "Approved by" sticker, that's $15,000 to the community.

If this process is repeated with 30 different gardening products, that's $450,000 in the cash register of seriousgardeners.com. What about newspaper ads and magazines? Helen of Soil can't use the "Approved by" sticker on ads in these print publications because they are the property of seriousgardeners.com. But Helen of Soil has measured in blind tests that the "Approved by" sticker sells 25 percent more bags of its soil additives in stores that bear the sticker than in stores that do not. Helen of Soil would be a fool not to pay the newspapers and magazines a premium for carrying the "Approved by" sticker, with seriousgardeners.com arranging to put itself in the middle and collect its ad agency fee of 15 percent.

Setting Up a Not-for-Profit

Online communities should set up not-for-profits in buddy-cars running alongside the main community, where grant money can be raised, and the grant money used to solve the pain of people voted on by the community. Contributors should be provided with links on the not-for-profit's web site. If the community is devoted to investors seeking to collaborate on investment techniques used by others, the gifts of the not-for-profit could go to associations that assist teenagers in learning about wealth creation, saving money, and the multiplier effect of investing.

Here's how not-for-profits work. First, Google "grants," and you'll find grants of all sorts. You can assign an eager employee to comb through them to find grants that apply to the issues in your online community. He then writes a number of grant applications. Some are awarded to your community, and some are not. A guild or foundation is formed under Internal Revenue Service Code

Section 501-C3, which grants the foundation not-for-profit status. The funds you take in from the grantors must be spent in the year you receive the money. A modest management fee of 10 percent of the funds can be paid to your community for managing the foundation. If you take in $200,000, the community will earn $20,000.

The foundation will need a board of directors to decide to whom the grant money should be given. The ideal recipients will be those people who might benefit the most in a related field. Using seriousgardeners.com as an example, the grant money can be spent on inner-city gardens, for instance. Naturally, you will want to post placards or small notices in the inner-city gardens that say "Funds Provided by Seriousgardeners.com." It could bring in more members.

Prepaid Credit Cards

The members will be paying for various things on the community, and you might consider creating a prepaid credit card in affiliation with Visa or MasterCard to send to the members when they sign up. The card will bear the name of the community, and it can be used outside the community for purchases, just like a normal credit card. As an accredited issuer of a prepaid credit card you will make money several ways. For instance, with each purchase, Visa will charge 3.5 percent on average, and kick back roughly a third of that to you. You can charge a set-up fee—after all, cards cost about $6 to produce—an annual management fee and a loading fee. If the member accesses her cash from an ATM, there is a fee of a dollar and a half, sometimes more, and the company that owns the ATM will send you approximately one-third of what it earns per use.

The prepaid credit card is also a loyalty builder. When it is used in public, nonmembers will see it and may ask the member about its name, and that could lead to a conversation about the things that the community does. Tip-jar payments can be made with the credit card, and members can buy kudos with it, or if they have collected a lot of kudos, and want to cash in, they can do so more easily with a community credit card.

Some communities have products. For instance, CollarFree.com, a community for clothing designers, sells back to the members the item of clothing that the members voted as best design each month. Designers can make $5,000 to $10,000 a month, and the members are delighted to wear something unique and best in its class.

In your social network, you can ask the members to design community-related products and have the members vote on the best. You can mass-produce them, and you can open a store in your community and sell the tee shirts, hats, bracelets, key chains, and the like that the members vote on—emblazoned with the community's logo. The products can be paid for with the community's credit card.

Another revenue channel to consider using with the credit card is to persuade merchants to give your members discounts when they purchase something using the prepaid credit card. The community can earn a slice of the discount as a fee for setting up the discount programs. That brings the total to six separate revenue channels with the prepaid credit card.

Build-in All 18 Revenue Channels: You now have 18 of the best revenue channels to build into your community. If you work with an outside firm to build and maintain your community, such as OneSite or Pluck, hand them this book and tell them you want all 18. They include the following:

Users group meetings
Subscription fees
Tip jar

Reputation management fees
Slice and dice the conversations
Port the community to mobile phones
The J.D. Powers business model
Synthetic currency/foreign exchange operation
Kudos
Sponsorships/ "Powered by. . ."
Affiliate ad networks
Setting up a not-for-profit
Prepaid credit cards—six separate cash flow channels

I'm going to give you another revenue channel: *branding*. It is massively disruptive and hugely profitable. Look for it in Chapter 6.

For now, a summary of the conversation is needed. I will do that by building a business model of a recommender online community that I call creditefficiencies.com.

Creditefficiencies.com: The Business Model

The heavy lifting in creating a business model is the list of assumptions behind the projections to the monthly cash flow statement. These have to be done granularly and updated continually because events change. Otherwise they are of little value. In what follows, I have created a list of assumptions to the three-year cash flow statement projections, and the cash flow statement projections themselves, to a recommender community. Where the three following conditions exist, a social network will likely thrive: *isolation* of the people most affected or at risk because they have no one to discuss the *complexity* of the issues with (and there are few things as complex as the fees charged by credit card issuers and the scoring of one's credit rating); and *regulation* (and as we know, the U.S. Congress was recently lobbied by the credit card industry to have the federal bankruptcy laws changed to benefit the lenders). I have chosen the credit card, credit reporting, and credit rating industries because of the opacity of the players and the consumers' need to know, plus the three-legged stool—*isolation, complexity,* and *regulation*. It could be a very successful social network. I call my community www.creditefficiencies.com.

The primary objective of creditefficiencies.com is to force the credit card issuers, the credit rating agencies, and Fair Isaac Corp. to *behave*—in the words of Max as he faced the wild things in his bedroom in Maurice Sendak's legendary children's book, *Where the Wild Things Are*: "be still." In my opinion, and that of just about everyone I have spoken with and every article I've read on the subject, there is a serious disconnect. I believe the most thorough thesis is "Illuminating the Obscure Model Called Fair Isaac," by Francisco Garcia, Anderson School of Management, UCLA, October 2006. The credit card issuers want us to use their cards as much as possible because they make their money only when we use them. They would like us to be a little bit late in paying our monthly bills and to exceed our borrowing limits so that they can charge us late and over-limit fees. But when that happens, they report our transgressions to the credit reporting agencies that pass along the negative information to Fair Isaac Corp. (FICO), which lowers our credit scores by (I understand this to be true) a significant percent per transgression.

Further, in the FICO algorithm, improvement in our credit scores occurs only when the credit balance in *all* of our credit cards is less than 35 percent of the authorized limit. In other words, the analysts at FICO have determined that if Sarah does not need more than $3,500 of a credit card with a $10,000 limit, she should have a significantly higher FICO score, other things being equal, than Emma, who needs $4,000 of a credit card with the same upper limit. Thus, the primary actors in the drama we know as building and maintaining a reputation for creditworthiness push us one way and pull us another, without working together or for our betterment, and without any clarity as to their objectives, but with considerable misinformation. It is the task of creditefficiencies .com to disrupt their business model and heal pain for credit-card-holders. The business model that we will build and execute has the following characteristics.

Rate, Review, and Recommend

As the founding entrepreneur of creditefficiencies.com, you will want to build your membership massively, to out the defectors and pretenders, and to report the transgressions of the corporations that make obscene profits, and whose top brass earn stratospheric salaries, as a result of not shooting straight with their customers.

To build members quickly, I recommend approaching the most important bloggers to report the news that creditefficiencies.com is up and running—you will need to launch a Web portal, of course, and install a dozen servers to handle the deluge of member sign-ups. Provide them with the PR blurb, which could be something like this: "If you have ever been treated unfairly by a credit card issuer or a credit reporting agency or if you believe your FICO score is too low, here is a new online community that is accepting members who will collaborate and work together to change the industry practices and business methods of credit card issuers and the credit rating and reporting industry."

Initially, the members should be permitted to join for free, except for a *reputation management* fee of $2 per month. This money will be used to find decoys and expose them in the community's newsletter. It will take some clever detective work to locate the decoys and wolves in sheep's underwear, but it can be done; and their names and the companies they work for should be published in the creditefficiencies.com newsletter and broadcast to conventional media. I discussed the method for outing wolves in sheep's clothing earlier in this chapter.

The second revenue source is the slicing and dicing of anonymized conversations regarding the credit card issuers, the credit reporting agencies, FICO, and some of the other alternative rating agencies. You can sell those ratings, rankings, and recommender reports to the members of the industry. Since they borrow so inexpensively—the prime rate is 4 1/2 percent, as I write this— and loan their money so dearly—19 percent plus penalty fees is not uncommon—they can afford a fairly steep price for the report; and it should be multiple-copy protected. If it is published in booklet form, be sure to squeeze the type toward the left side of the pages to prevent photocopying. A price of $10,000 per copy per month sounds about right.

Tip Jar

The newsletter needs stories. The stories that are submitted should be on point; such as one woman's fearless battles with Equifax to remove a dozen untrue statements about her in Equifax's credit report; or one man's year-long battle with TransUnion to remove false tax liens from his credit report; and a college students' story of receiving 30 unsolicited credit cards upon entering the university and his attempts to get rid of them. Readers who learn something from these stories should be encouraged to pay tips to the authors via the community's prepaid credit card with a $10 minimum established at the outset.

The community's owner-operator will keep 30 percent of the tip money and the happy author will receive 70 percent.

Given these three revenue sources, and assuming an exponential membership growth rate, as opposed to a linear one, after month six, see Exhibit 1.2 for the kind of monthly cash flow statement creditefficiencies.com generates:

EXHIBIT 1.2   Creditefficiencies.com 12-Month Cash Flow Statement Projections

($000s)

	Mo. 1	Mo. 2	Mo. 3	Mo. 4	Mo. 5	Mo. 6	Mo. 7	Mo. 8	Mo. 9	Mo. 10	Mo. 11	Mo. 12	Total Yr. 1
Cum. Members	5,000	7,500	10,000	12,500	15,000	20,000	40,000	60,000	89,000	120,000	160,000	200,000	200,000
Report Buyers	-	-	1	3	5	7	12	18	24	30	36	42	42
Revenues:													
Rep. Mang. Fees	10	15	20	25	30	40	80	120	160	240	320	400	1,460
Newsletter Sales	-	-	10	30	50	70	120	180	240	300	360	420	1,780
Tip Jar	-	-	-	2	2	3	4	8	12	16	24	32	103
Total Revenues	10	15	32	57	83	114	208	312	416	564	712	860	3,343
Optg. Expenses:													
Systems Engs.[a]	-	7	7	7	14	14	21	28	35	35	35	42	245
Newsletter Pubs.[b]	21	21	21	42	42	42	84	84	84	168	168	168	945
Marketing Mgmt.[c]	36	36	36	36	36	36	36	36	36	36	36	36	432
Purchase Servers	-	11	-	5	-	-	5	-	-	5	-	10	36
Travel, Telecom	-	2	3	4	5	6	7	8	9	10	11	12	77
Office Rent, Misc.	5	5	5	5	5	5	5	5	5	5	5	5	60
Professional	20	20	5	-	-	-	-	-	-	-	-	10	55
Unspecified	10	10	2	2	2	2	2	5	5	5	5	10	60
Total Optg. Expenses	112	102	85	104	105	118	163	174	180	290	276	294	1,863
Net Optg. Income	(102)	(87)	(53)	(47)	(22)	4	45	138	236	274	436	566	1,480

[a] There is one systems engineer for every four servers for every 20,000 members. A systems engineer is paid $72,000 a year plus benefits at 20 percent.

[b] There are initially three employees who gather data for the newsletter, doubling every six months, and paid the same as systems engineers. They also produce the reports.

[c] The founder and a marketing team run the Company at a cost of $10,000 per person/mo plus benefits at 20 percent.

In this set of just 12-month cash flow statement projections we learn several things. First, the cumulative cash loss is $311,000, which occurs for the first five months of operation, before break-even is reached. Since Murphy's Law applies to all start-ups, it is wise to raise several dollars more than the projected cumulative cash deficit. Raising $400,000 from family, friends, and angel investors would be the wise move.

We also learn that creditefficiencies.com builds cash profitability very fast. In months 6 through 12, it throws off $1.7 million in free cash flow, enough to expand into some interesting areas that are described in Chapter 5—enough to make multiple online community launches as described in Chapter 4.

Silver's Law Applies

For those of you who read *Smart Start-Ups*, I have a fondness for testing business models against formulae that I have used over the years as an angel investor. Assuming you have read *Smart Start-Ups*, I will test the model against the formulae. First, let's see what numeric value the creditefficiencies.com business model produces.

The principal test is whether the problem is a large one, and in this particular case it is not only large, but one of the largest ones in existence. There are 140 million holders of credit cards in the United States. Approximately 40 percent of the holders pay their balances in full every month, which brings down the market size to 84 million individuals. Eighty-four million concerned people is a large homogeneous market by any standards. The second test is the elegance of the solution, which refers to the nonduplicability or first-to-market of the solution and the uniqueness of its means of delivery. An online community that rates, reviews, and recommends credit card issuers and rating agencies can be started by many people; thus, the uniqueness of the means of delivering the solution to the problem will separate the winner from the losers. Third is the quality of the entrepreneurial team, and that is an open item. Executing this particular business model will require skill and guts, because credit cards are major profit centers for banks and the sole profit centers for nonbank issuers; and the issuers will not welcome this particular community with hugs and kisses. If you prefer softball to hardball, this Bud is not for you.

The next eight factors, which I call the *Demonstrable Economic Justification* factors, include the following:

1. *Existence of a Large Number of Receivers:* This opportunity speaks to the awareness of the problem by 84 million credit card holders and by people who want to know how to improve their FICO score. It would seem that every cardholder and potential home buyer would like to save money and have a higher credit rating. As a former commercial banker, I quote a Wall Street homily: "If one has to explain his credit worthiness it is presumed to be in doubt." Accordingly, good credit is something everyone wants because it is a mark of respect.

2. *Homogeneity of Receivers:* Will the consumers accept a standardized solution, or will it need to be customized? Most problems will be of a standard nature, but in the event of a requirement for a customized solution, the community will respond. A member with a problem comparable to one experienced by another member will find a helpful solution—worthy of a tip-jar payment—from the experienced member.

3. *Existence of Qualified Receivers:* Will there be a cost involved in finding new members? Yes, at first, because there will be distrust of any new solution to a problem involving something as private as credit. For instance, we know that people fear identity theft, and creditefficiencies.com may be perceived as a place where one's credit could be stolen. Thus, the community

may need a spokesperson, or a board of advisors composed of some of the top names in finance. Imagine the power of a Paul Volcker endorsement! That could cost a small percentage of ownership, but it would be equity well spent.

4. *Existence of Competent Providers:* The wisdom of crowds is going to be the solution provider, and the solutions they provide will be based on their experience in dealing with sudden increases in interest rates and having the credit reporting agencies remove false information. Only Equifax is a publicly held U. S. company, and therefore open to filing grievances within the judicial system and the New York Stock Exchange. TransUnion and Experian are conveniently based in foreign countries, and immune from conventional dispute resolution mechanisms.

5. *Absence of Institutional Barriers to Entry:* There is no regulatory authority that blocks the oligopsony power of online communities. The playground is perfectly level for creditefficiencies.com to build a reputable business at a relatively low cost.

6. *The "Hey, It Really Works" Factor:* You will need some early, documentable successes in order to make creditefficiencies.com gain traction in its early months. To do this, the community will need some experienced, battle-scarred members to guide some new, timid members through the process of taking their troubles with credit card companies and credit rating agencies and tossing their problems out to the wisdom of crowds to come up with battle plans. When the new members obtain roll-backs of fees and interest rate decreases, and especially when they get untrue statements removed from their credit reports, they can write stories for the community newsletter and possibly earn kudos points and tip-jar money for their journalistic efforts.

7. *Invisibility:* You will want to operate this community very quietly for several reasons. The formula could be adopted by a competitor. The enemy will want to regard you as a tiny blip on their radar. If the enemy thinks you are well-organized and well-funded, they could arm themselves before you are ready for the Battle of the Bulge. Do not talk to the press; operate out of cheap offices in an out-of-the-way location; and shred all paperwork at the end of the day. Always remember that you are attacking the most profitable departments of large banks, and they will do everything imaginable to crush you. Some of them book "Litigation" as a revenue line item!

8. *Optimum Price/Cost Factor:* The community's cost of goods sold will be borne largely by the community's members, except for the cost of servers and the salaries of systems engineers who write programs and maintain the servers. If you charge a reputation management fee going in of $2 per member per month, and if you persuade some of the leading blogs to bring in the members and build an initial base in the first few months of 10,000 average daily users, I would consider that a good start.

Bear in mind that creditefficiencies.com is a David v. Goliath community. You will need to arm David, the community, with slings and arrows, to add to his smooth stone and slingshot. You might consider doing an early disruptive event against one of the credit card issuers or credit rating agencies, in which a success is scored against them; then broadcast the news throughout the Internet with the goal of attracting a threat from the enemy to bring legal action. This is known as Little Richard's Law and its premise is that rock 'n' roll became even more popular in the 1960s when preachers spoke out against it from the pulpits and songs such as "Wake Up Little Susie," by the Everly Brothers, were banned in Massachusetts for being too suggestive. (For more on Little Richard's Law, see *Smart Startups*.)

You say that I preached about remaining invisible, but I was talking about bragging to the press and capturing the interest of the media about membership growth, capturing a major celebrity endorser, or talking about the size of your community. Little Richard's Law is all about getting under the skin of the industry you are trying to disrupt. It is the "irritation" business model: Attack a "brand," the "brand" sues, and your community is famous.

Strength will come to you by taking continual small but important steps that score wins for your members and losses for the opponents. Carefulness will trump creativity in the early days, and new capital will flow in from reputation management fees and tip-jar payments and from utilizing some of the glue factors described in Chapter 5. Initial angel capital of $400,000 or thereabouts should be sufficient to hire a staff of system engineers, build out the community's Web portal, and persuade bloggers to announce the formation of creditefficiencies.com. Your goal is to disrupt an industry that has obfuscated the tautology of their terms and conditions beyond comprehensibility and has thus taken advantage of consumers for dozens of years. You can heal pain for nearly 100 million people. The task is awesome, but the rewards can be very significant.

2

Your Recommender Community as Theater

THE INTERNET AND, MORE PRECISELY, the emergence of the recommender social network, are powerful economic forces that are requiring existing industrial corporations to develop a fundamental new competency. They must return to their entrepreneurial mission statements and become authentic.

This is not an easy task. Large corporations must master a new discipline to ensure continued success, and that discipline is to capture and hold, by action and deed, a reputation of trustworthiness. Advertisements will not carry the load of building a convincing, credible escutcheon of authenticity because in the Age of Experience, ads will not be persuaders of consumer choice; the wisdom of crowds will.

The Age of Experience

The economics of the developed countries evolve, or perhaps the word is "lurch," from interval to interval as new drivers emerge to reduce the cost of goods produced and marketed. With each evolution, managers have to learn new tools, or they are forced out of the game. The assembly line invented by Henry Ford ushered in the era of quality goods mass-produced to fulfill every whim and desire. For about 50 years, managers moved up the income and responsibility ladder, and decorated their walls with attestations that notarized their mastery of mass-producing boxes of consumer nondurables, ticky-tacky houses, insurance salesmen, cars and trucks, and dishwashers, to mention a few items. *Six Sigma, zero defects,* and *kaizen* were the corporate battle cries.

The Age of Quality was replaced with the Age of Service when the semiconductor was commercialized in the late 1960s at about the time when the world became saturated with goods. We needed parts distributors, more retailers, interior designers, lawn care specialists, security systems to maintain and protect our goods, and cable TV systems to provide us with 600 channels serving us with myriad forms of entertainment.

The Internet made possible the "social transactional framework"—a phrase coined by Yochai Benkler—and the introduction of the Age of Experience. Let's examine Benkler's hypothesis. It is a given that all of us want the highest quality goods and services at the lowest transaction cost. By the latter, we mean the actual fixed cost plus the variable costs of delivery, installation, operation, maintenance, service, and upgrades.

Market economics are being radically changed because "…social transactional frameworks are likely to be substantially less expensive than market transactions for pooling large numbers of discrete, small increments of the excess capacity of personal computer processors, hard drives, and network connections that make up the physical capital base of the networked information economy," wrote Benkler in *The Wealth of Networks,* the bible for parishioners of recommender social networks.

Benkler's hypothesis says that Beatrice Jones, sitting at her $499.99 Dell Inspiron computer in Chattanooga, Tennessee, after joining the gardeners' online community, seriousgardeners.com, and typing in her pleasing experiences with HappyLadybug, a soil enhancer product, can influence more purchases of HappyLadybug by expending a few pennies with her ISP and amortizing the $499.99 she spent with Dell over five years, than can the producer of HappyLadybug that spent $50 million to advertise it.

Beatrice Jones has a larger capital base of authenticity than the producer of HappyLadybug will ever have. Why? Because Ms. Jones is a card-carrying member of seriousgardeners.com, whose reviews, rankings, and recommendations, stored in her community locker for other members to read, are *trusted*. Her words are of purest strands of gold. She is the Florence Nightingale of soil enhancement in the eyes of her fellow gardeners. Her tip jar is overflowing.

And there are millions of Beatrice Joneses—or soon will be—in tens of thousands of recommender social networks typing their truths about consumer products and services that blast to smithereens customer response software (CRM), which is the service tool that the corporate world has inflicted on consumers like a plague of locusts over the last 10 years. The experiences that consumers have had with millions of products and services, and tens of thousands of providers of products and services, will soon be available on recommender social networks for anyone to read and act on accordingly. The power shift is from the Age of Mass-Produced Quality, and the introduction of continually degrading service by ill-trained customer service specialists sitting in Indian call centers, to the Age of Experience, where consumers tell stories about their experiences with cough medicines, disposable diapers, daycare centers, auto insurers, attorneys, mortgage lenders, bank service charges, dry cleaners, security systems, and credit card issuers, among others. We are returning to simpler times—to times when truth stood for something important.

Experience as Theater

Before the Internet and before institutional angel and venture capital, entrepreneurs introduced their products and services by theatrical means. Today's entrepreneurs, particularly those who are conceiving web applications such as social networks, have no recollection of the creative attempts to fill auditoriums of customers for their products and services because they were not yet born. Today's social network entrepreneurs operate more linearly during the launch and thereby raise the cost of the launch, thus wasting precious capital, because they don't know about the ingenuity of entrepreneurs during the 1950s and 1960s, before the Internet and before the abundance of start-up capital.

Let's look at company names. They no longer stand for anything. In the Age of Experience, a company name should say what the experience is at the online community the entrepreneur is launching. *Ning* does not mean what Ning purports to do, which is to house low-cost, do-it-yourself social networks. At the moment, it trumps the other well-known builders and maintainers of online communities, OneSite and KickApps on compete.com—where numbers of unique visitors per month are measured comparatively—by a wide margin (see Exhibit 2.1).

EXHIBIT 2.1   Unique Visitors per Month as Measured by Compete.com

Online Community Builders	May 2008
Ning.com	2,164,670
OneSite.com	425,870
KickApps.com	130,237
Pluck.com	31,363
Mzinga.com	13,929
Smallworldlabs.com	8,064

But Ning raised $60 million as a start-up, at a valuation of $560 million post-funding, for a cost per unique visitor of $27.70. KickApps, Pluck, and Mzinga have taken in an average of $35 million in capital. Thus, their "uniques" cost them $269.23, $1,115.96, and $2,517.99 apiece. OneSite has bootstrapped its launch, and so its "uniques" have the lowest transaction cost: zero.

OneSite has the more descriptive name. "Site" refers to web site. "One" refers to the one place to come. OneSite's web site says what it does in plain words. It says: "Web sites are being replaced in importance by social networks, and we build and maintain them for entrepreneurs and existing companies."

Because it is based in Oklahoma City, OneSite is too far from the home offices of most venture capitalists, and thus it couldn't attract the Sequoias or Kleiner Perkinses, who prefer their portfolio companies to be within an hour's drive of Silicon Valley.

Ning was founded by Marc Andreessen, one of the most successful entrepreneurs of the Age of Experience. He founded Netscape and Opsware (née Loudcloud), which were acquired respectively for $4.2 billion by AOL, and $1.6 billion by Hewlett-Packard. Andreessen, who is 39 years old, is an angel investor in more than 20 companies including Digg, Twitter, Plazes, and Netribes. When he says "jump" to Silicon Valley venture capitalists, they ask "how high?" He answered, "Five hundred million dollar pre-money valuation for Ning, my next venture." That valuation, to my way of thinking, is as preposterous as Microsoft paying $240 million to own 1.6 percent of Facebook in 2007, which valued Facebook at $15 billion.

When a start-up requires $60 million and an emerging growth company without much in the way of revenues raises $240 million, to my mind neither one has thought through its business model very thoroughly, and both are probably thinking that advertisements will be their primary revenue channel. I predict that Facebook will acquire Ning, because both communities are apartment houses of do-it-yourself social networks and web applications, and they are overcrowded and difficult to navigate.

Names

Curtis L. Carlson, founder of Gold Bond Stamp Company in 1938, and subsequently Radisson Hotels & Resorts, Regent Cruises, Carlson Marketing, TGI Friday, and Carlson Wagonlit Travel Services, among others, selected "Gold Bond Stamp Company" as a trade name for the following reason. "If you have funds to advertise," Carlson told *Success* magazine, "you should pick an unusual name or coin a name—such as Lux for soap—so through your advertising, people will always identify the name with your product. But if you have no funds to advertise, as in my case, you should pick a name that will itself inspire the buyer to think what you want him to think about your product." Because he had no money, Carlson drew up his own incorporation papers and tried to persuade mom-and-pop grocers that they could combat the giant chains with trading stamps. Carlson's wife, Arleene, donned a drum majorette's costume and worked the floors of the local groceries to capture the interest of customers. That's theater!

Henry Taub and Joe Taub, the founders of Automatic Data Processing, Inc., the leading supplier of payroll processing and accounting services to millions of companies, a service based on trust if there ever was one, clearly described its service offering with its name. *Processing* is a verb that clearly describes the activity of the company.

When Sam Shoen founded what would become the largest one-way truck and trailer rental business in the country, he chose the name "U-Haul Systems" to describe exactly what his company did. Shoen persuaded gasoline station owners throughout the country to handle the rentals and paperwork needs for a fraction of the action. The U-Haul network has been a difficult one for competitors to pierce since its founding in 1945, because it is essentially community-based; that is, the members are the gasoline station owners and the nearby neighbors who have done trust-based business with them for many years. A brilliant model. If Shoen hypothetically were directing a play called *U-Haul Systems* his actors were and still are gasoline station owners and people hauling their possessions from place to place. Theater equals community.

The name "Nike" was conceived the night before the company's name had to be imprinted on boxes to be shipped to the 1972 Olympic trials. Employee Jeff Johnson came up with the name "Niké," who is the goddess of Victory in Greek mythology. She is most always depicted with wings in statues and paintings. The name has served the company well, as it triumphs in many sports. Nike bears the solid-gold stamp of authenticity and trust as does its namesake.

Kemmons Wilson founded Holiday Inns of America, Inc. in 1952 when he found, on an automobile trip with his family, that he could beat the competition by offering services they didn't. Holiday Inns launched by offering reasonable prices (children stayed for free), dog kennels, air-conditioning, 24-hour phone service in every room, ice and soft-drink machines in the halls, a swimming pool, and doctors, dentists, babysitters, and clergymen on call. He took the name from a popular Bing Crosby movie called *Holiday Inn*, released in 1942.

Trading stamps marketed by a drum majorette dancing in grocery stores: musical theater. ADP says, "Let us process your data, while you do something you enjoy." Gasoline station owners renting boxes, on wheels to traveling families: ballet. Winged victory on shoe boxes, putting the customer on the winner's podium at the Olympics: pure opera. Holiday Inn: The words practically spell "fun." Names are important.

Design

"At Sony, we assume that all products of our competitors have basically the same technology, price, performance, and features. Design is the only thing that differentiates one product from another," said Norio Ohiga, the former chairman of Sony Corp.

In his breakthrough book, *A Whole New Mind*, David H. Pink writes, "For every percent of sales invested in product design, a company's sales and profit rise by an average of 3 to 4 percent, according to research at the London Business School."

Bayerische Motoren Werke AG, otherwise known as BMW, consistently outperforms all other car manufactures in vital statistics such as profitability and return to stockholders. Its head of marketing was quoted as saying, "We don't make automobiles. We make moving works of art that express the driver's love of quality."

If you really want to learn about how to design your community's home page, pick up a copy of *The Perfect Thing: How the iPod Shuffles Commerce, Culture, and Coolness*, by Steven Levy. It is not only the tale of the birth of the iPod, which is a full-blown cultural phenomenon and disrupter of the music industry, but it is a story of the migration from the breakthrough Sony Walkman to the granularly detailed design and redesign of the iPod.

Levy tells this story about the search for "cool." He was interviewing Yossic Vardi, the developer of the first instant messaging program, who said, "I don't know if it's true or not but I heard that when the Japanese wanted to create the Lexus, they took three hundred engineers and they told them, 'Go and see why the Mercedes is cool!' And they defined all these very implicit, tacit things in the Mercedes, like, for instance, the click of the door." Levy goes on to report the detailed engineering required to produce the simple "click" of a Mercedes door.

Apple is viewed as a consistently cool company. That is largely due to Steven Jobs's fanatical approach to developing and maintaining an image of coolness. Remember the Think Different ad campaign? It never identified the heroes by name—Picasso, Alfred Hitchcock, Muhammad Ali, Gandhi, John Lennon, Bob Dylan. When it came to designing the iPod, Jobs was intensely involved in the white earphone cord. Levy describes the result thus: "The white earphone cords—painstakingly drawn frame by frame by post production artists—would shake wildly, a serpentine invitation to the aural bacchanalia provided to those who partook of the iPod drug."

Entrepreneurs and artists have many things in common, principally their desire to overcome a deprivation by saving some portion of humanity with a joyful creation. In this respect, both are problem solvers. The artist tries to solve some of life's problems by expressing solutions on canvas. The entrepreneur focuses intensively on one problem, formulating and reformulating it until he or she is ready to pull out one huge canvas and begin painting. Both species, the artist and the entrepreneur, are individualists, unconventional, sensitive, imaginative, intense, complex, driven, and creative. Although one could argue the differences, the similarities are greater in numbers. Therefore, the study of creativity among artists by Jacob Getzels and Mihaly Csikszentmihalyi has a bearing on our investigation of the entrepreneurial process.

The participants in the study were young male art students. Each participant first completed a still life for the researchers based on an arrangement he made from a collection of objects provided. Afterward, the artist answered several questions.

One question was: "Could any of the elements in your drawing be eliminated or altered without destroying its character?" The objective of the investigation was to determine whether a student considered his work fixed or flexible.

The answers to this question enabled Getzels and Csikszentmihalyi to draw a correlation between ability and recognition of the possibility of change. A panel of judges rated each artist's drawing.

Those who received the highest ratings overall were the ones who said their work might be changed. A follow-up study seven years later by the same investigators indicated that more success had come to the artists who earlier had seen the possibility for change.

Certainly the committed artist is a perfectionist. Why then would there be a correlation between willingness to change a finished piece and artistic success? Quite simply, perfection is too costly to achieve. Rather than spend the time and effort to perfect, a successful artist will spend less time and be satisfied. Satisfaction is the goal in problem finding, not perfection. The potential entrepreneur should free his or her mind of any notions of finding the perfect problem and supplying that demand curve with a perfect solution. In the entrepreneurial process, random collisions are the norm.

Getzels and Csikszentmihalyi learned something about the work methods of the artists and their professional success. The most effective artists displayed these work traits: In arranging the objects that they were preparing to paint, they manipulated them more, moved them about and then rearranged them more, moved the mechanical parts more, and chose more unusual objects. They tended not to have a predetermined theme in mind prior to beginning to paint, but discovered arrangements through handling the objects.

As they began drawing, they more often rearranged or substituted objects, changed paper, switched media, and transformed the scene and subject of the drawing. The final structure of the drawing tended to emerge later rather than earlier. These artists reported that they tried to develop the drawing beyond the physical objects. In addition, after completing the drawing, they admitted that it could be altered without destroying its character.

The researchers regarded the artists' problem finding as a measure of creativity. The more creative artists, who indeed had become more successful seven years later, devoted more time to problem formulation. The actual drawing, or problem-solving activity, remained open to further changes in matters such as the arrangement of the objects, which seemed to have been settled during the problem-finding stage. That is, the more creative artists often found new problem formulations even while working from the original one.

The late George Quist, a venture capitalist who began in the early 1970s and provided seed capital to some of the most successful entrepreneurs in the country, said essentially the same thing: "The road to success isn't always going to be straight. The smart guy will realize there will be a lot of turns—changes in the market, for instance. The honest entrepreneur can face up to that."

Theater

Theater has existed since the beginning of time as a result of the human tendency for storytelling. It has evolved from speech to gesture, to music, dance, and spectacle. Online communities are the venue, and storytelling is the dominant means of presenting. Many online community founders seem to want to control the storytelling events, and crowd their pages with self-adulation and *amour-propre*, conceit and vanity.

Google has an inspired home page. Two words stand out: "Google" and "Search." Brilliant.

A number of entrepreneurs have used theater to get their message across.

McDonald's Corp. was initially based on the desire of teenagers to drive their cars into drive-ins, with music blaring from their car radios, ordering hamburgers and milkshakes, and jitterbugging in the open spaces. Musical theater.

Here's a slogan that should be adopted by one of the recommender social networks: "You meet the nicest people on a Honda." Soichiro Honda, the founder of the eponymous company, introduced his motorbike to the American marketplace with that slogan in 1962. The motorbike had a reputation of being suitable for beefy men in black leather jackets and oil-stained jeans when Honda introduced its step-through "Cub." The brilliant ad gave the Cub mass-market appeal and it sold like hotcakes.

Roger Horchow, founder of the Horchow Collection in Dallas in 1973, the first mail-order catalog company not associated with a famous retailer, discovered that people rarely return gift items if their initials are on them. He built a $100 million gifts business on that simple notion. How easy it would be to reward social network members with a community-logoed product with their name on it. What a loyalty builder.

"Vanity well fed is benevolent. Vanity hungry is spiteful," wrote Mason Cooley, an American aphorist, who taught English at Columbia University from 1959 to 1988. Putting members' names on gifts they buy in your community store means they are more likely to show them off.

Sheldon Adelson produced the most successful theatrical event in the computer industry: COMDEX. Adelson purchased *Communications User* magazine in 1972. He attended a condominium conversion trade show in 1972 and learned that the show's sponsor also published a magazine. Like the 16-year-old vending machine owner who began selling ice cream bars when he went to collect his nickels, Adelson immediately visualized trade shows as "living magazines" or "magazines in the flesh." In 1973, after changing the name of his magazine to *Data Communications User*, Adelson sponsored his first trade show, the Data Communications Interface show, where manufacturers of data processing equipment exhibited their products for end users. He learned the trade show business thoroughly over the next six years. In 1979, as the personal computer was emerging, Adelson saw the need for a trade show aimed at dealers and distributors. Eight months after the idea for the first COMDEX, Adelson's dealer-oriented trade show rolled out, and it did not stop rolling until he sold it in the late 1990s for more than $2 billion.

But, perhaps the most theatrical of all pre-Internet entrepreneurs was Roy H. Parks. He was born hard scrabble poor on a farm in Dobson, North Carolina, but his father was able to send the four children to college. His first job came in 1931, while Parks was still a student at North Carolina State University in Raleigh.

"I saw a want ad in *The News and Observer*.... Someone was looking for a young man to do some writing. Those days many ads like that were come-ons, and I wanted to be sure this one was legitimate. The ad said to write Box 731, Raleigh, so I did. But I put the letter in a pink envelope. Then I went to the post office the next morning and waited till I saw someone take the pink envelope out of the box. Then I eased over and found out who was offering the job." It was the North Carolina Cotton Growers Association. Anticipating that he would be interviewed for the job, "I had bought myself a white cotton suit and showed up for the interview wearing it."

The Cotton Growers Association was reluctant to hire him. So Parks told his prospective employer, "I have my own typewriter and don't need an office. If you just find me a table in a corner somewhere, I'd work three months for nothing."

Parks was hired and he stayed with the Association for 11 years, editing a magazine, and taking care of public relations and sales promotion. One day, out of the blue, Parks received an invitation from Dr. H.E. Babcock, head of a farmers' cooperative called GLF, now known as Agway, to come to Ithaca, New York, to discuss an opportunity. Parks replied that he would move only to have his own business. "Young man," Dr. Babcock said, "you just bought it."

"What business did I buy?" Park asked.

"Your own ad agency," he replied. "If you need money, we'll lend it to you." Dr. Babcock was also Chairman of the Board of Trustees at Cornell University.

Parks grew the business steadily and wisely, sticking to advertising for farm businesses. He opened branches in five other cities and expanded to 125 employees in six years. Then, "I fell on my face."

"My mistake was getting into political advertising, where we did several campaigns for Tom Dewey, including appeals for the farm and small town vote in 1948." When Truman beat Dewey, many clients identified Parks' firm as a loser and switched to other agencies. Parks had to come up with a new idea.

The farm cooperatives had shown the need to Parks for a consumer brand name of their own. Extensive market research indicated to Parks the enormous consumer appeal of the name "Duncan Hines". At that time, Hines was America's most famous restaurant reviewer, and the author of guidebooks that rated restaurants. Parks felt that a line of Duncan Hines food products would be potent. There were two obstacles, however: (1) Hines had never permitted his name to be used and (2) Parks didn't know how to get to Hines. To prepare for his eventual meeting with Hines, Parks read everything he could find on the man. He knew that Hines did not want to license his name for the wealth it might bring him. Parks was introduced to Hines by a mutual friend, and Hines asked the young man: "So you're going to make me a millionaire?" Parks said, "No . . . [but] you can help upgrade American eating habits." Knowing also that Hines never endorsed anything, Parks came prepared to the meeting with completely finished Duncan Hines labels, in full color, on dummy cans, cartons, and jars so that Hines could see what the concept looked like. They shook hands on a deal.

Parks and Hines began product planning and testing immediately. All products underwent blind tests before market introduction to assure consistency from one product to the next. Rigid quality control standards were set by Hines, and he saw that the company's manufacturers met those standards.

In the meantime, Parks's farm cooperative clients backed out of their commitment to pay some of the up-front costs for an interest in the profits. Parks had to raise money quickly, which he did from family and friends and by pulling cash out of his advertising agency and letting it slide away. To save production and shipping costs, Parks mailed the labels to the packages rather than the other way around. Soon after its introduction, Duncan Hines cake mix captured a 48 percent market share. Pillsbury, Swans Down, Aunt Jemima, and Betty Crocker bravely took the hit. As Parks says, "We could never outspend those giants—so we out-thought them."

Duncan Hines was the first cake mix to be advertised on television. In the late 1940s, Mr. Hines acted in the commercials, which was also a first in consumer products advertising. Hines-Parks Foods was also the first company to use four-color ads in newspapers. Parks also used outdoor ads to remind the housewife of the commercial she had seen the previous evening on television. And here is where it gets exciting. Parks took Hines on the road, talking mayors and governors into declaring Duncan Hines Days and presenting him with keys to the city. The Duncan Hines Days generally ended with a big dinner, to which the governor, the mayor, city bigwigs, and the key chain store buyers were invited, along with their wives. The latter were presented with a corsage and an autographed *Duncan Hines Cookbook* on arrival. Parks instructed his people to sell nothing at the party. "Next day was another story," says Parks.

With distribution in 23 states and 120 different cake mixes, the Duncan Hines brand was second in sales among all brands by the mid 1950s.

Parks left the Duncan Hines business in 1953 to return to his first love—journalism. He spoke frequently at business schools, providing students with these seven rules for entrepreneurial success:

1. Pay attention to detail.
2. Get things done on time.
3. Delegate to others all that they can handle as well or better.
4. Use showmanship, imagination, dramatize what you are doing.
5. Take action. If you have the facts and a little common sense, and you *move*, you've got a better than 50 percent chance of being right.
6. Do your business homework.
7. Reinvest your profits—but always keep a liquid position.

Go Hollywood

One-dimensional online communities are doomed to failure. Need an example? Ford Motor Company's reliance on its 150 series of trucks and SUVs when the price of gasoline at the pump rose to more than $4. Multiple marketing channels must be developed for the survival of the community. Think like a Hollywood movie producer. They make money in many ways; and as one who has been to the Cannes Film Festival several times selling foreign rights, I can assure you they have a lot of fun doing it.

U.S. theatrical distribution
Foreign theatrical distribution
DVD sales

Mobile phone, iPod sales soon to come
U.S. network television
U.S. cable television
U.S. independent television stations
Military and in-flight
Book rights
Product placements
Other rights such as games, toys, calendars, beach blankets, bed linens, and robots

Back in the day when I raised capital for movies I had a better database of what these 11 channels brought into the movie producers' cash register in dollars and percentages of total revenues. I recall that General Mills paid $300,000 for Rocky to feed his young son Wheaties in Rocky II, and grunt the words, "Here, the Breakfast of Champions." And the Darth Vader mask sold roughly 25,000 units at $40 apiece, in conjunction with the launch of *Star Wars*.

The Creative Process

The creative process in entrepreneurship has not been investigated thoroughly, and is only now being studied in artists and scientists. However, the studies by D.N. Perkins present a large body of ideas from which we can draw to learn more about the creative process as it applies to entrepreneurs. D.N. Perkins provides us with good principles of creativity for actors, artists, and social network entrepreneurs.

Try to be original. If you want to be creative, you should try to build into any outcomes that property of originality. This sounds almost too silly to mention, but I don't think so, and have given some reasons for that. Many supposedly creative pursuits like painting can be pursued in very humdrum ways. Major figures in the arts and the sciences often were certainly trying to be original. Creativity is less an ability and more a way of organizing your abilities toward ends that demand invention.

Find the problem. Early in an endeavor, explore alternatives freely, only gradually converging on a defined course of action and keeping even that flexibility revisable. The evidence is that creative people do this. The principle makes all the more sense because later on in the process is often too late—too late to build in originality or intensity or other qualities you might want.

Strive for objectivity. Problems of accurately and objectively monitoring progress pervade creative activity. The judgment of the moment may prove different tomorrow; the revisions of today may prove wrong in a week. Manufacturers have adopted many strategies to cope with the caprice of their own impressions, such as setting a product aside for a while. Also, learning to fashion products that have a potent meaning for others as well as for yourself is a complex process. Beginning with the child's first experiences of language and picturing, the problem of reaching others reappears throughout human growth in more subtle guises, which plague even the expert maker. Sometimes, it may be best to ignore such hazards and freewheel for a while. But if you always freewheel, you never really take advantage of your own best judgment.

Search as necessary and prudent. That is, explore alternatives when you have to, because the present option has failed, or when you had better do so, because taking the obvious course commits substantial resources that might be better spent. Of course, the conventional advice of many works on creativity is to explore many alternatives routinely.

Try, but don't expect, to be right the first time. The research found that people trade quality for quantity. Aiming at fluency, they lower the standards governing their production of ideas, select imperfectly, and achieve no net gain. This is advice against doing just that. Instead, ask your mind to deliver up the best possible results in the first place. Notice that this does not mean fussing over initial drafts, trying to make them perfect by editing in process. Neither does this say that the results will be right the first time. They likely will need revision, maybe extensive revision—and maybe the wastebasket and a new start. This is why you have to adopt a paradoxical attitude: while being perfectly comfortable about filing short. The point is to bias the quick unconscious mechanisms that assemble the words we say, the gestures we make, toward doing as much of the work as possible and leaving as little as possible for deliberate revisions. To put it another way: Ask yourself for what you really want—you may get it, or at least some of it.

Make use of noticing. The ability to notice patterns relevant to a problem is one of the most powerful gifts we have. This can be put to work deliberately by contemplating things connected to the quest. Suppose, for example, you are designing an innovative house and need ideas. Walk around a conventional house, and see what transformations suggest themselves. Or examine a conventional house in the mind's eye with the same objective. The latter can be particularly powerful, and the mind's eye takes a willing traveler to places inconvenient for the body or billfold. Often books on creativity recommend exposure to seemingly unrelated things to stimulate ideas. This certainly sometimes works, as Darwin, Archimedes, and others have taught us. But, in my experience and judgment, sensitive scrutiny of things related to the task at hand usually yields a richer harvest of ideas.

When stuck, change the problem. Early on in the space race, NASA spent much time and effort seeking a metal robot strong enough to withstand the heat of reentry and to protect the astronauts. The endeavor failed. At some point, a clever person changed the problem. The real problem was to protect the astronauts, and perhaps this could be done without a material that could withstand reentry. The solution, the ablative heat shield, had characteristics just opposite to those originally sought. Rather than withstanding the heat, it slowly burnt away and carried the heat away from the vehicle. Let me generalize this and similar examples into a heartening principle. Any problem can be solved—if you change the problem into a related one that solves the real issue. So ask yourself what the real problem is, and what constraints have to be met and which ones can be changed or sacrificed. (There may be more than one way of formulating the real problem.)

When confused, employ concrete representations. Darwin's notebooks, Beethoven's sketchbooks, a poet's drafts, an architect's plans all are ways of externalizing thought in process. They pin down ideas to the reality of paper and prevent them from shifting or fading in memory. All of us do this at one time or another. However, despite such habits, we may not realize that making thought concrete can help to cure confusion on nearly any occasion. When paths lead this way and that and refuse to show the way, circle back, make notes, make drawings, make models. Think aloud or form vivid mental images, for such internal concreteness helps some, too.

Practice in a context. Most advice on how to be creative urges the learner to apply it everywhere. However, sometimes "everywhere" is so indefinite and daunting a notion that it turns into nowhere. When people want to improve their creativity, my suggestion is for them to choose some likely activity, then undertake it—often—and try hard to be more creative every time they try. Focus breeds progress. No need to hold back in other activities, but be sure of one.

Invent your behavior. That is, people should think about, criticize, revise, and devise the way they do things important to them.

Too often, inventive thinking is limited to the customary objects of invention—poems, theories, essays, advertising campaigns, and what not. But part of the art of invention is to select unusual objects of invention—objects like your own behavior. This isn't just nice; it's needed. Performances do not necessarily improve, even when you do them frequently. Indeed, it's common lore that people often end up practicing and entrenching their mistakes.

These, then, are some possible plans up front, another contribution to the young and hopeful technology of thought. These principles and others like them try to define and impart the limited but very real edge, which is about the best you can hope for from very general principles. Perhaps the plans mentioned are hard to take, at least as advice. Their prescription is too broad, too much in the direction of telling the daydreamer to pay attention or the grind to daydream more. Just what they mean in particular cases and how one persuades oneself to behave accordingly are serious questions. But take them as general principles and take seriously the problem of translating them into practice, and then they make more sense. There's no reason why the right principles (whether these suggestions are right or not) have to be as easy as a recipe for boiling water.

The elegant solution comes to the deeply committed entrepreneur, not as the result of invention but frequently after working with all of the elements of the problem, much as Monet painted the church facade at different times during the day in order to capture sunlight on canvas. Clearly he did not produce the sunlight precisely, but he did produce some beautiful impressions of sunlight. Edwin H. Land did not invent instant photography as a solution to the problem of delayed film development time. He worked for 14 years on the problem of headlight glare and the possible solutions from polarizing light. His daughter asked him one day while he was snapping her photograph with a Kodak, why it took so long to get her picture back. Land was struck by the question and sought the answer within the field of polarizing light.

Chester Carlson, a patent attorney, came up with the idea for xerography as a solution to his particular need to make neater copies of patent applications than were available with a mimeograph. Fred Smith named his overnight small package courier Federal Express because he believed that the Federal Reserve Bank would be his most important customer due to their clear need to move money around rapidly. They did not become a very significant customer. In many cases, the solution fits into the problem randomly, but effectively, because the entrepreneur recognizes that accidental fit and causes it to happen.

The *Playbill* Solution

Upon entering a theatrical production, you are handed a magazine. If it's a Broadway play, the magazine is named *Playbill*. The sale of information concerning the theatrical production, ballet, symphony, or opera often produces greater wealth than does the whole compendium of that year's theatrical productions.

Although every industry has two or three magazines or newsletters that slice and dice and publish the goings on of their industry, the social network industry has none. Well, there are several cheaply knocked out online newsletters, but no major magazine has emerged. This opportunity is so big you could drive a Kenworthy truck through it. That's exactly what Patrick J. McGovern did 40 years ago when a similar opportunity emerged.

Patrick J. McGovern, 68, is the most successful marketer of information since Paul Revere. I wrote a book in 1982, called *UpFront Financing*, whose premise is that there are roughly 20 ways to finance a start-up company, but the least expensive is customer financing. Moreover, if entrepreneurs select areas where there is a lack of information about the nature of the problem and the quality of the solutions, and where buyers and sellers have a great deal of uncertainty about each other, the entrepreneurs can sell information to both of them. In fact, in most new markets, the first multimillionaire is the journalist, the person who sells information about the market. Subscribers will pay in advance for the information, and so will market research clients, so the journalist need not dilute his equity ownership by selling some of his stock.

If this sounds too hypothetical, note that IDG is the world's leading technology media, research, and trade show production company. It had revenues of $3.02 billion in 2007 generated by 13,640 employees worldwide. IDG reaches 200 million customers in 92 countries. More than 86 million unique visitors visit IDG's 45 web sites each month. It offers a 24-hour global technology news service supported by more than 2,000 journalists. IDG produces over 750 trade shows a year in 55 countries, including MacWorld Conference & Expo and LinuxWorld Conference & Expo.

When McGovern was 15 years old, he became so interested in computers that he decided to build a version of his own. "I spent about $20 of my newspaper route money and wired up a computer system with carpet tacks and bell wire, plywood boards, and flashlight bulbs . . . and made a machine that played tic-tac-toe in a way that was unbeatable." McGovern told a reporter for *Business New Hampshire*. "Except, I found people didn't like to be unsuccessful continuously, so I made it make a mistake every 40th move, so in somewhat unpredictable style, they could win occasionally." The tic-tac-toe machine earned McGovern a scholarship to the Massachusetts Institute of Technology (MIT).

At MIT, McGovern noticed he was not alone in his fascination with the computer. "People would wait six or seven hours in the early morning, 4 or 5 A.M. to get access to one of those large vacuum tube machines or transistor machines that were around then." His own interest grew and after graduation he accepted a position as associate editor of *Computers and Automation*, one of the early computer magazines.

While honing his reporting skills for six years, McGovern became convinced that most computer companies knew little about who was buying computers and what they did with them. He approached the head of Univac with a proposal to "organize a market research program and create a census that [would indicate] where all the computers are and how they're being used." McGovern says the executive liked the idea and agreed that most computer manufacturers had only limited information about the marketplace. McGovern asked for $7,000 or $8,000 to do the study.

The Univac executive replied, "That's completely unrealistic."

McGovern lowered the price of the project to $5,000. But he had misread the Univac officer's concerns. McGovern says the executive told him, "You don't understand. I couldn't get anyone to use information that was too cheap. Charge at least $12,000 and sell it to a lot of other companies, too."

McGovern immediately wrote a proposal and mailed it to Univac and the other major computer manufacturers. Within a week, "I got probably $70,000 of prepayments." Nearly every company had forwarded a $6,000 advance toward the project."

With money in hand, McGovern founded IDG. Within three years, the business was grossing an annual $600,000, and McGovern was searching for new ideas that would expand the company's base of business.

One idea was *Computerworld*, a trade publication for the computer industry. "We found that managers of computer systems were very unaware of what people were achieving with computers. So we thought that it would be useful for them to get rapid-access information about the new products and services."

The decision to launch *Computerworld* was made shortly before a Boston trade show in 1967. Faced with a two-week deadline, McGovern and his staff scrambled to produce a 16-page tabloid and subscription materials. Originally, he intended to call the magazine *Computer World News,* but this was shortened when at the last moment, the typographer could not fit the entire name across the page. At the trade show, McGovern was able to attract enough subscribers to publish. As with his first research project, he got his money up front.

Other journalistic entrepreneurs have entered the computer industry, but none has achieved IDG's level of success. What is McGovern doing differently? His senior officials call him "one of the nicest men on the face of the earth." His entrepreneurial energy is unabated. McGovern still travels 60 percent of the time: high for a manager, normal for an entrepreneur. McGovern says that he enjoys spotting needs that IDG can fill, while leaving the publishing and market research operations in the hands of capable managers. Other insights about McGovern are that he sleeps very little, works relentlessly, remembers small details about people, and does not let people know what he is thinking. McGovern is a pure play in entrepreneurship.

If you believe as I do, that the social network market has the potential to become bigger than the computer market, then why don't you become the publisher of its leading magazine and the impresario of its most important trade show?

3

Mimic the Bakers and Copy Starbucks

The Discovery of Bread

Picture, if you will, the discovery of bread. The owners of fields— let's call them wheat fields—best suited for the growing of the *best wheat* that makes the most delicious bread will benefit the most because they will have the lowest production costs and the highest cash flow. They can charge high rents and sales prices. The owners of grassland, not particularly well suited for growing wheat that becomes tasty bread, will benefit the second most, when the prime land is fully rented or sold. The owners of scrubland that must be cleared first and for which deeper wells must be dug to irrigate the land for the production of wheat will benefit marginally, when the better farming sites are fully planted.

With more and more entrepreneurs jumping in to fill the enormous demand for bread, the price of bread falls. The clever bakers invent derivatives such as Danish pasty, Jewish matzoh, British scones, French baguettes, Italian cheese bread, Mexican tortillas, and the like to satisfy every imaginable taste bud. These derivative products require peripherals such as raisins, fruit, cinnamon, sesame seeds, and so forth, which are additions to the cost of goods sold, thus boosting the price to the consumer.

Now, assume that bread is the Internet and the wheat-based derivatives of bread—cakes and pastries—are the more expensive items, such as mobile phones that are connected by wireless access. These two discoveries, recent inventions—the Internet and the mobile phone—are the modern equivalent of bread and pastries. They are massively disrupting the means by which consumers get their news, entertainment, work-related data, and interpersonal communications; but their platforms are not scarce. They are ubiquitous.

The Ubiquity of Bread

The synonyms of the word *bread* are more in number than for any other word in *Roget's*.

They include the noun form:

Synonyms: bagel, bannock, brewis, brioche, brown, bun, challah, chapatti, corn, croissant, crouton, diet, dough, fare, flatbread, food, french, gluten, hardtack, heel, host, italian, lite, load, malt, matzo, nan, pita, potato, pumpernickel, puri, roll, rye, sippet, soda, sop, sourdough, squaw, staple, stolen, sustenance, toast, wheat, white, whole-grain, zwieback;

Something to be eaten: aliment, comestible, diet, edible, esculent, fare, foodstuff, meat, nourishment, nurture, nutriments, nutrition, pabulum, pap, provender, provisions, sustenance, victual;

That which sustains the mind or spirit: aliment, nourishment, nutriment, pabulum, pap, sustenance;

The means needed to support life: alimentation, alimony, bread and butter, keep, livelihood, maintenance, subsistence, support, sustenance, upkeep; and

Something, such as coins or printed bills, used as a medium of exchange: cash, currency, lucre.

The extraordinary importance of bread from biblical times when Moses granted every Jew in Canaan an equal portion of land, with free disposition over it (that's the right to buy and sell) forward to Solon's transformation of Athens into an agrarian democracy (639–559 B.C.) was the foundation on which most religions and constitutions of democratic societies are based. Bread means the need for equal access to land. The Fourth Amendment to the United States Constitution—"The right of the people to be secure in their persons, houses, papers, and effects"—is testament to that fact. We know that Hamilton and Madison, the principal authors of the Constitution, were serious students of Cicero, Socrates, and Virgil.

The utility of bread as sustenance, the value of wheat as animal feed, and the functionality of bread as currency and a means to enable trade between seafaring countries such as Greece and fertile countries such as Egypt, provided bread with its unique role in the history of civilization. For more on the subject, read H.E. Jacob's *Six Thousand Years of Bread* (New York: Skyhorse Publishing, 2007).

The New Bread

The Internet, I contend, is the new bread. New laws will have to be passed and new legislation written to protect information about the cognitive strengths and weaknesses of children that our schools record, and that search engines can break into. The same applies to our health records, credit scores, and other personal information, which, if made public, could be more destructive than losing our land. We need a new Moses; we need another Solon to enlighten the government officials to maintain Net neutrality and protect our children's school records, our health records, and our

creditworthiness records with three new constitutional amend-
ments. That is an important task of online communities.

The Internet has enabled the social network. The social network has the transformative power of bread. The social network
has the *authenticity* of bread. And we are the new bakers. Our
social networks are the offshoots of bread. They are the bagels,
cakes, challahs, scones, babas, puffs, pies, strudels, baklavas, dan-
ishes, delicacies, éclairs, tarts, flans, fritters, goodies, schnekens,
and phyllos of our day. It is our common task as social network pioneers to maintain their quality, goodness, taste, essence, and utility
in ceremonial events and authenticity in order to make the social
network the transformative force that it is destined to become.

Authenticity

There are many commentators on the subject of authenticity
as the new "real" in consumer marketing. James H. Gilmore and
B. Joseph Pine II, in *Authenticity: What Consumers Really Want*
(Cambridge: Harvard Business School Press, 2007), write about
"our view of advancing sensibilities from availability (scarcity) to
cost and quality (abundance), to authenticity".

David Lewis and Darren Bridger, in *The Soul of the New
Consumer: Authenticity—What We Buy and Why in the New Economy*
(London: Nicholas Brealey Publishing, 2000), see the developed
world having moved "from scarcity to abundance—from abundance
to authenticity." Lewis and Bridger associate this new demand for
authenticity with "New Consumers" whom they define as indi-
vidualistic, involved, independent, well-informed in their tastes
and behaviors, and transcending national boundaries, ages, ethnic
groups, and incomes.

In *The Rise of the Creative Class: And How It's Transforming
Work, Leisure, Community and Everyday Life* (New York: Basic

Books, 2002), Richard Florida similarly observes "the emergence of a new social class that desires more active, authentic and participatory experiences in more authentic, indigenous or organic venues."

Florida cites Paul H. Ray, who segments society into three groups: Traditional, Modern, and Cultural Creative in *The Cultural Creatives: How 50 Million People Are Changing the World* (New York: Three Rivers Press, 2002). Ray says the Cultural Creatives "invented the current interest in personal authenticity in America."

David Boyle, author of *Authenticity: Brands, Fakes, Spin and Lust for Real Life* (London: Flamingo, 2003), labels Ray's Cultural Creatives with his own term, the "New Realists." He claims that the New Realists represent "a little less than half the British population, and just under a quarter of the American population," and are the ones "driving the demand for authenticity."

The appeal, all of these authors write, is for the *real*. Bakers have served up the real and the authentic for 6,000 years. They have handed off the baton to social network entrepreneurs.

Authentic and Nonauthentic Social Networks

Entrepreneur-launched social networks have an enormous advantage over enterprise-launched social networks. The former are trustworthy. The latter lost their trustworthiness years ago when their marketing deceptions, union-busting, oil spillage, nine-figure golden parachutes to exiled senior managers, and other shameful acts removed their emblems of authenticity.

But they persist. They build online communities, although not ones in which the members speak their truths—except for a certain chauvinistic species of truth.

Bazaarvoice was formed three years ago by Austin, Texas, serial entrepreneur Brett Hurt, on the premise that retailers will want to know what consumers think about them and they will need a means for those conversations to be captured, sliced and diced, and sent to them on a regular basis. Bazaarvoice builds online communities for large retailers such as Wal-Mart and Best Buy and moderates the conversations that occur on the forums of these retailers, keeping out sexist or racist comments, and providing their clients with reports on subjects such as unpleasantness at the check-out line and which boom-box cases scratch most frequently, thus making them nonsaleable, and which boxes of tissues appear crushed and unattractive all the time. Bazaarvoice has over 250 retail chain clients, and it is growing rapidly. It charges its customers a monthly fee based on traffic and page views.

When a consumer visits Wal-Mart's online community, it is actually visiting Bazaarvoice, which runs that online community for Wal-Mart. Why would Wal-Mart subcontract its community to an upstart Austin, Texas, company? Because it wants to get a summary of the conversations held on the community, and it doesn't want to read every rating, review, or recommendation every day. That would be too time-consuming. It gladly pays Bazaarvoice to do that job. Bazaarvoice has raised $19.5 million in venture capital and has 250 employees with offices in London, Paris, and Singapore.

There are a handful of corporations and enterprises that have built and maintained authentic and trustworthy brands. Consumerist.com ranks the 2008 winners, as shown in Exhibit 3.1.

I visited the winners' web sites, and some of them are trust-building. For instance, Adidas asks visitors to review its products, and presumably the posted scores are accurate. Despite its high trustworthiness status, Adidas' web site has far fewer unique visitors per month than does Nike, which did not make the list: 299,800 versus 1,821,172 for Nike, according to compete.com, as of June 2008.

Most of the 15 brands on the consumerist.com list are products makers, a handful are retailers, and one is an airline. Noticeable

EXHIBIT 3.1   Consumerist.com's 15 Most Trusted Brands

1. Apple
2. Trader Joe's
3. Jet Blue
4. In-N-Out Burger
5. Ben & Jerry's
6. Whole Foods
7. Adidas
8. American Apparel
9. Target
10. H&M Clothing
11. Levi's
12. Volkswagen
13. Converse
14. Vitamin Water
15. Red Stripe Jamaican Beer

in their absence are banks, mutual funds, insurance companies, travel agencies, matchmakers, health-care providers, pharmaceutical companies, computer and software companies, engineering service companies, restaurant chains, legal services firms, chemical producers, and agricultural firms.

It is more likely that a start-up recommender online community will survive and thrive in industries that are considered less trustworthy or authentic.

The new, trust-based online social network model has authenticity going for it because of its "rookieness." It works like this.

In the new model, the users control what is baked in the fields—the content. The users market the content to other users who wish to collaborate about the content and who will pay to search the content useful to the community, share the content with others in the community, and are rewarded by the community for exceptionally useful stories, videos, news, or data.

The paradigm shift is a matter of control: The consumers of the content are also the generators of the content, and they displace many previous content generators. The branded advertiser is displaced, except for minor sponsorship placements, on community Web portals that permit them. The nonbranded advertiser can still use Google and Yahoo to attract clientele when there is a click-through next to a relevant word. But that is a scrubland market because of its high cost of finding customers.

Disruption on this scale is titanic. Owners of and employees of well-known consumer brands and their ad agencies are losing control, indeed, losing their *raison d'être*, and the purposes of their jobs; and the skills that they once thought were marketable are becoming worth very little. They may attempt to launch online communities, but they lack the trust that entrepreneurs have, and most of their efforts are risible and are tossed aside by the marketplace.

The disruption is on a similar scale for the owners and employees of media companies, those that entertain us and provide us with news. They do not own the wheat fields—or in the current genre, the "pipes"—or the gadgets that connect to the pipes—PCs, PDAs, mobile phones, or iPhones—nor do they own the software that directs the flow of user-generated videos and news over the pipes and to the users' handsets. They own the content, but it is not user-generated, and user-generated content is what the community joiners demand and spend more and more time sorting through and collaborating on.

The Baker's Knife

How many years of life do the old media have left? Unless they reinvent themselves in a community format, they have five years left before they become as dead as Bear Stearns. Trying to save them is like trying to catch a falling knife. The average age of their viewers/readers/listeners is around 60, and they are dying off without replacements.

The millennials are growing older each year, but they get most of their news and entertainment from the Internet and their mobile phones. The millennials don't mind advertising as a form of payment to the bread and pastry producers; however, as the bread and pastry consumers become the producers of content as well, they will develop reciprocal forms of compensation that will obviate the role of advertising as a necessary means of compensating the producer. The reciprocal forms of payment include reputation management fees, the sale of anonymized conversations to the big brands, subscription fees, tip jars, kudos, product sales, commissions for bringing new members into the community, affinity credit cards, and more.

Everyone with Internet access or a mobile phone, from 8 years old (the demographic that joins Club Penguin) to 80 years old, will belong to between 5 and 25 online and recommender online communities by 2011. That means that the greatest demand curve of the next three years is for creators of online recommender communities to build the platforms to enable consumers to tell their stories, share information, show videos, and search for scarce information.

The Wedding Cake

Have you been to a wedding lately? Did the bride and groom cut the wedding cake? Was that event the center of attention, and did the dancing begin shortly afterward? Disassociate yourself from the wedding for a moment and ask yourself, "How did a cake become the center piece of weddings?" The answer lies with the relentless creativity of bakers.

Many social networks are one-dimensional, designed by geeks in their twenties who think linearly rather than peripherally. Often shy and inner-directed, these founders of social networks see a wedding cake as just a wedding cake. The bakers of old saw an opportunity to make the cake a central part of weddings, indeed a celebratory bit of pastry that can cost $500 to $5,000. That is a huge mark-up on wheat, sugar, labor, and the energy consumed by the oven. To survive and thrive in the online recommender community world, founding entrepreneurs must learn to copy any and all entrepreneurs who have gone before them and thrived in industries of nonscarce resources.

Learning to Observe

How does one do that? It is called *learning to observe* things around you. There is ceremony everywhere, but very little of it in social networks. For example, many highly successful and revolutionary companies and countries have and have had mission statements. The American Revolution produced some amazing mission statements, beginning with Thomas Jefferson's "We hold these truths to be self-evident" in the Declaration of Independence. Observe Abraham Lincoln's incredible mission statement in his Gettysburg Address, "that government of the people, by the people, and for the people shall not perish from the earth." How magnificently a variation on these two phrases might work for an online recommender community. Something like this: "A truthful community of, by, and for its members." Or let the members recommend mission statements, and then vote for their favorites.

There are other famous quotes from cultural leaders that can be put up on the community's web site home page on a rotating basis. Here are several that offer encouragement:

Actions may not always bring happiness; but there is not happiness without action.

—Benjamin Disraeli.

All the beautiful sentiments in the world weigh less than a single lovely action.

—J.R. Lovell, from "Among My Books."

You shall not muzzle an ox when it is treading out the grain.

—1 Corinthians, 9:7–9

Nothing will be attempted if all possible objections must be overcome.

—Samuel Johnson.

By perseverance the snail reaches the Ark.

—C. H. Spurgeon.

In kindergarten class, there is a lot of emphasis placed on "growth" and "growing." Kindergarten is where most new social networks are at this point in time, relative to upper grades. Therefore, there is much for you to learn by observing a day at kindergarten class.

Watch Us Grow should be an important page in your community's Web portal. On this page, you might have your graphic artists create a map of the United States, or North America, or a country in which your community intends to grow its membership. As a new member joins, place a pin in the region of the country where she lives. As additional members sign on, add more pins for their regions. Make text announcements about how one region is growing faster than another. Award prizes to members who bring in the greatest number of new members. Announce the growth rate continually. You might consider using a thermometer with the membership goal at the top, and placing it prominently on the Watch Us Grow page.

Personality

The word derives from the Latin verb *personare,* to sound through. Personality is not a page of text. It is a particular sound. A violin concerto played by Itzhak Perlman has personality. A country and western song by Ray Charles has personality. And bakers have personality that they infuse into their delicious and beautifully crafted gastronomical wonders. The wedding cake didn't become the centerpiece of weddings on its own. Salesmanship sounding through must have had a lot to do with it. If sardine salesmen were as personable as bakers, brides and grooms might be placing sardines into each other's mouths at weddings.

Your community will need to develop a warm and appealing personality for your social network in order to distinguish it and set it apart from competitive communities. This can be done with sound, or sound and lovable characters, or sound plus friendly visuals that are associated with the motif of your community.

Starbucks Strategy of Target Pricing

The Internet is ubiquitous, the Web is almost free to build a business on, servers cost as little as $500, and start-up social networking entrepreneurs can put 25 credit cards together, cash in their Bar Mitzvah Israel bonds or First Communion checks, and become a disruptive force offering a pain-solver to millions of members inside of 90 days. There is no scarcity on the Internet. So, how does one price the pain-solver of the product or service that she offers at her social network? Put a little differently, if Sol and his team launch the community airborneallergies.com, and Joan and her team launch peoplewithallergies.com, and five other entrepreneurs do the same, all in the same week, which one is the most likely to survive, thrive, and create the greatest wealth for its owners? The answer is this: the one who understands the Starbucks business model.

There is no scarcity of coffee, right? There is no scarcity of coffee shops, right? Like the Internet or virgin wheat lands before the discovery of bread, coffee is ubiquitous. If that's the case, then consumers hold the bargaining power when they have a taste for a cup of coffee. Thus, the price of a cup of coffee should be relatively low. If there were a freeze in Brazil, Colombia, and Kenya, and all the coffee bushes were killed, then coffee drinkers would see prices rise, because their favorite morning liquid would be scarce.

In *The Undercover Economist,* the economist Tim Harford, whom you may know from his NPR interviews, describes the concept of target pricing to explain how Starbucks disrupted the existing coffee shops and solved our pain for needing to feel special. Starbucks employs what economists call "first-degree price discrimination" to evaluate each customer as an individual and charge each according to how much he or she is willing to pay.

The strategy is one that I used as chairman of the Temple Beth Shalom Building Fund in Santa Fe, New Mexico, when we needed a new building. I would visit a couple in their home, for instance, and after we talked for a few minutes, I would pull out a blank index card and hold it up at roughly the middle of my face as if I were reading it. Then I would say, "Mr. and Mrs. Steinberg, our committee, made up of your fellow congregants, have come up with a number—a dollar amount—that they think you would be comfortable pledging to the Temple building fund."

Then I would pause and look at them with a knowing smile. As I looked down, they would look at each other. They were dying to know the dollar amount that I supposedly had written on the index card. But I wasn't telling. Peer pressure was at work. The desire to tell the community, "We're wealthier than you think we are," always produced a pledge greater than the number that the committee estimated. If they estimated $20,000, I always got a pledge of $25,000 or $30,000. Because I knew what Howard Schultz knew about target pricing, he created a wonderful business called Starbucks and Santa Fe's Jewish community got a new building.

When I visit Starbucks in DeVargas Mall in Santa Fe, the price list looks like this:

Hot Chocolate	$2.20
Cappuccino	$2.55
Caffé Mocha	$2.75
White Chocolate Mocha	$3.20
20 oz. Cappuccino	$3.40

Or, to translate:

Hot Chocolate—no frills	$2.20
Cappuccino—no frills	$2.55
Mix them together—I feel special	$2.75
Use different powder—I feel very special	$3.20
Make it huge—I feel greedy	$3.40

Starbucks isn't merely seeking to offer a variety of alternatives to customers. It's also trying to give customers every opportunity to signal that they've not been looking at the price. It doesn't cost much more to make a larger cup, to use flavored syrup, or to add chocolate powder or a squirt of whipped cream. Every single product on the menu above costs Starbucks almost the same to produce, down to the odd nickel or two.

Does this mean that Starbucks is overcharging all of its customers? No. If so, a regular cappuccino or hot chocolate would cost $3.30, and you could have all the frills you wanted for a dime. Perhaps Starbucks would like to do that, but they can't force price-sensitive customers to pay those prices. By charging wildly different prices for products that have largely the same cost, Starbucks is able to smoke out customers who are less sensitive about the price. Starbucks doesn't have a way to identify lavish customers perfectly, so it invites them to hang themselves with a choice of luxurious ropes. (*See* Tim Harford, *The Undercover Economist* [New York: Random House, 2007] p. 32.)

Let Them Eat Pastries

The creative bakers—those who diversified into pastries, and Howard Schultz, who persuades us to pay over $3 for a feel-good cup of coffee—solved their dilemmas of gaining economic leverage in a market of nonscarcity. Applying that to the service that Sol, Joan, and others offer on their social networks for allergy sufferers works like this.

Step One: No advertising is permitted, because it obfuscates the ultimate purpose of your social network, that only the truth may be spoken here.

Step Two: Inform the members that they are expected to pay a tip to the member who provides them with the best solution to their allergy. Assign different values to the tip minimums, for instance:

Drippy Nose	$5.00
Headache and Congestion Vanished	$10.00
Could Finally Get Out of Bed	$15.00
Able to Get Back to Work	$100.00
Congestion-Free for 30 Days	$250.00

Step Three: Capture the data, the conversations, and the information being shared; slice and dice it; and sell it to the producers of drugs that are supposed to combat allergies for high prices, some as high as $10,000 per quarterly report. All of them will buy the reports. They have to, because they assume that their competitors will purchase them, and if you get 25 corporate customers paying $40,000 apiece per year, you have made $1 million in almost gross-equals-net dollars.

Although the earliest social networks get their launch value by attracting massive memberships, the ones with highest revenues per member, are, at the end of the day, the social networks that have found the empty chairs in this musical chairs game of recommender social networks. It is the best execution of the cleverest business models that will decide the winners.

4

Why Not Start Five Simultaneously?

ON A SCALE OF 10, WHERE 10 REPRESENTS the easiest and 1 stands for the most difficult, launching an online community rates a 10. The most difficult kind of company to launch is a biotech business, because of the enormous skill required, the huge amounts of capital needed, and the regulation walls to climb. Capital equipment companies rate a 2, because of the skills, capital, and precision component manufacturing needed.

But for online communities, one need merely find a market in which a large number of people have a homogeneous pain, are not obtaining quality information that would relieve their pain, and are willing to pay the relatively minor cost of joining a community and collaborating with others who share the same pain and would gain some form of relief in talking about it. The cost of goods sold in online communities is borne by members, thus revenues drop all the way down to the operating expenses line—salaries, payroll taxes, insurance, marketing expenses, rent, utilities, professional fees, and consumables. Operating expenses should run at around 20 to 30 percent of revenues, once the social network is operating at $2.5 million in revenues or more, producing a Net Operating

Income/Revenues ratio of 70 to 80 percent. That is a phenomenal return on revenues.

Name any industry other than recommender social networks that can achieve an NOI/Revs ratio of 70 to 80 percent, and a return on stockholders, investment of 100 percent by the second or third year, and I'll name my next child after you, no matter what its gender. *There hasn't been a wealth-creating opportunity to compare with recommender online communities in the history of modern economics.*

Okay, so you say that the myriad products, such as scones and pecan rolls, that emerged following the invention of wheat and bread had a higher cost of goods sold than did wheat; thus the logic doesn't work. First, the Web is ubiquitous, whereas prime wheat fields are limited, after which farmers turned to grassland and scrubland, pulling quality and taste down with them. Second, there is a capital equipment requirement in the bakery business, which doesn't exist in the online community business.

What bakers have going for them, as we learned in the previous chapter, is how brilliantly they wangled their products into many celebratory and religious events across cultural and religious barriers. Diplomats should carry a bakers' dozen with them and distribute the goodies at every difficult negotiation. But, I digress. Online communities are relatively easy to launch; no particular skill is required; the people with pain suffer their pain homogeneously—no customizing required; the members pay for the cost of goods sold; there are more than 18 cash flow channels; no venture capital is needed; and online communities have the highest potential return on revenues and stockholders' investment of any business in modern economics.

So, Why Not Launch Several?

Pain is greatest in the broad arena of health care. There are several fascinating new online communities in this space, and three of my favorites are hystersisters.com, patientslikeme.com, and sermo .com. As of June 2008, they ranked about equally in numbers of unique visitors per month, to wit:

hystersisters.com	51,278
patientslikeme.com	48,456
sermo.com	44,813

Two of the three are trending up—patientslikeme.com and sermo.com—while hystersisters.com has been relatively flat, as is shown in Exhibit 4.1, from compete.com.

Each of these communities is extraordinary in many ways, and they provide valuable services to people in need. Hystersisters.com had 215,000 members in September 2008 and 2,257,022 posts. Kathy Kelley, a former school teacher, founded the company in Denton, TX, in 1998, long before there was a Web.

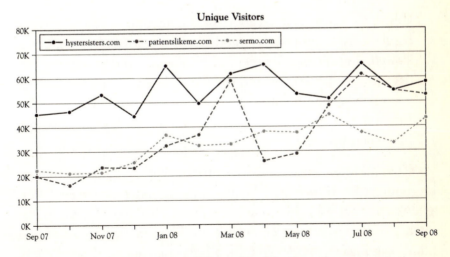

EXHIBIT 4.1   Comparison of Three Health-Care Communities

"We began as a bulletin board service," Kelley said. "After we evolved into an online community, I left teaching, and hired a couple of people and we've grown every year. Thirty volunteer members now monitor the conversations." Its main revenue channel is advertising and its secondary revenue channel is conducting clinical trials for pharmaceutical companies. The pain solver it provides is conversations among its members concerning the myriad aspects of having a hysterectomy. But the members do not leave the community after they have found the pain-solvers they came for. They make lifelong friends and discuss their recipes, family events, children, grandchildren, and life issues. It screams for a recommender page where medical products, hospitals, physicians, and other products or services are reviewed, rated, and recommended and then sliced and diced into reports and sold to the pharmaceutical industry.

Patientslikeme.com collects people with serious diseases including ALS/motorneuron disease, anxiety, bipolar, depression, HIV/AIDS, multiple sclerosis, OCD, Parkinson's disease, PMA, PLS, and PTSD. Its Openness Philosophy, posted prominently on its site, reads as follows:

> Currently, most health-care data is inaccessible due to privacy regulations or proprietary tactics. . . . As a result, research is slowed, and the development of breakthrough treatments takes decades. . . . When you and thousands like you share your data, you open up the health-care system. . . . We believe that the Internet can democratize patient data and accelerate research like never before.

Communities such as patientslikeme.com require divulging quite a bit of personal health information to strangers. But, as one member told the *New York Times*, "I know it sounds like really personal information, but it's not like I'm putting my phone number up," says Jennifer Jodoin, a hotel manager in Palm Beach,

Florida, who has changed her multiple sclerosis medication based on information gleaned at patientslikeme. "I'm not posting my address and saying, 'Come on by.' It's an exchange of information to get help and to give help."

That pretty much defines *pragmatism*, and it exemplifies these strategic information-for-benefit exchanges that people often make, like taking a blood test to get life insurance or consenting to a background check to secure a new job. Only now, at places like patientslikeme, information has a currency that's far more liquid than ever. Converted into data and bundled with information from those like us, private information can be invested for both immediate gains and long-term returns.

Patientslikeme.com appears to generate its revenue from foundation grants. It lists partnerships with the Accelerated Cure Project (multiple sclerosis), the Myelin Repair Foundation (multiple sclerosis), and the Milton S. Hershey Medical Center at Penn State University (ALS). It raised $5 million in February 2007 from Collaborative Seed and Growth Partners, LLC and Invus, LP. Earlier investors include Commerce Net and Omidyar Network (Pierre Omidyar founded eBay).

Now we turn to the online community that physicians are increasingly turning to for the wisdom of their peers: sermo.com. Its mission statement is this:

> We are a practicing community of 65,000 physicians who exchange clinical insights, observations and review cases in real time—all the time.

One would have thought that a large health-care corporation or the Centers for Disease Control would have captured this space—gathering physicians into a self-help community—but they missed the boat.

Dr. Daniel Palestrant, founder and chief executive of Sermo, says doctors' increasing sense of isolation was one of the most unexpected findings that was made when launching his social networking site a year ago. "Golf is a thing of the past; even doctors, lounges are things of the past. What was shocking to me was these doctors described themselves as 'lonely.'"

But that is changing as doctors are now linking themselves and their practice of medicine in new ways with technology that is more often associated with teenagers than surgeons.

This shift is highlighted in the current collective discussion among Sermo's online community of more than 65,000 physician members on what to call themselves. So far, they prefer "Sermoans." The Sermoans are medical in the MySpace age. And it's not just the younger set fresh from medical school. The attraction of belonging and the ability to publish or broadcast their professional pursuits to a distinct and interactive online social community and receive feedback is grabbing the older, busiest doctors the most.

Sermo, which verifies each member's credentials, is free to join for doctors, whose profiles can range from minimal biographical information to photos and personal details. Its business model rests on two fundamentals: no advertising and open, unedited interactions between members.

For instance, a doctor posts a medical case and others help to work on the problem. Other discussions can expose conflicts of interest in doctors, seek emotional support, or ask for guidance on hiring and firing office employees. "The wisdom of crowds dictates these things. It's startling how effectively this happens," Dr. Palestrant says.

Sermo makes its money by anonymizing the conversations of its physician-members, slicing and dicing them, and selling the conversations as reports to pharmaceutical companies such as

Pfizer and others. Dr. Michael Berkowitz, head of global medicine at Pfizer, says, "We learn how best our medicines may be used [from the physician-members] and how that knowledge of our medicines may be generated."

Launched in September 2006, Sermo has raised approximately $39 million in venture capital, most recently in September 2007, $26.7 million from Legg Mason, the Baltimore asset manager, and Allen & Co., the New York merchant bank known for its commanding position in entertainment investments.

Analysis of Three Business Models

The three popular online communities that we have just reviewed have relatively thin business models and could, I believe, benefit from the prescriptions in this book.

Hystersisters generates revenues from ads and clinical tests in which its members participate; patientslikeme.com receives grants; and sermo.com uses the slice-and-dice revenue model. Having one revenue channel is a risky proposition because if the one goes away, you have none. Google derives most of its revenues from advertising, which enables it to offer search for free. But, the current recession and its concomitant reduction in ad spending has hurt Google. Its stock price has fallen by 60 percent from a mid-2007 high of $747.24 per share. In my opinion, Google needs to add revenue channels away from advertising, a fickle channel. They bought dodgeball.com, a mobile social network, but haven't expanded it very much. The creativity of Google workers is and always has been at a high level, but it needs focus.

Additionally, the three communities could easily multiply into many. Hystersisters could expand into other areas of female sexual dysfunctions and gynecological problems, and copy Sermo's slice-and-dice revenue model, for each of its communities.

Patientslikeme could split up into 10 different communities—one for ALS, another for bipolar, a third for Parkinson's disease—and so on. The infomercial revenue channel comes immediately to mind for patientslikeme. Local TV channels would love to broadcast stories of how chronically ill people are thriving through sharing.

And Sermo could bifurcate into physician specialties—orthopedists, heart specialists, dermatologists, and more. These strategic moves, added to a multiplication of revenue channels to some of the 18 recommended herein, would add enormous revenue jumps to all of the primary and spin-off communities, accompanied by greater benefits to shareholders. Moreover, it is a good competition-blocker move. Remember the wheat-to-Internet analogy. Anyone can enter the online community business with family, friends, and angel capital. There are many prime grasslands to occupy, and if new entrants adopt multiple revenue channels and execute their business models elegantly, they can grab market share from established icons such as hystersisters, patientslikeme and sermo. It has been done before. Remember Netscape?

When your community has captured the high end of its market, as sermo.com apparently has, and does not block the low end, a competitor will take the low end—call it scrubland—with a lot of capital and sales smarts, and eat its way up to the high end until it takes a chunk of that as well. GoDaddy did it with the web-hosting market.

Ideas for Multiple Launches

Rodeo comes to mind. Let's tackle a huge market that is just sitting there, dying for a social network. Some background first.

Rodeo is a sport that arose out of the working practices of cattle herding in Spain, Mexico, and later the United States, Canada,

South America, and Australia. It was based on the skills required of the working *vaqueros*, and later, cowboys, in what today is the western United States, western Canada, and northern Mexico. Today it is a sporting event that consists of several different timed and judged events that involve cattle and horses and are designed to test the skill and speed of the human cowboy and cowgirl athletes who participate.

Rodeo, particularly popular today in the Canadian province of Alberta and throughout the western United States, is the official state sport of Wyoming and Texas.

In North America, the traditional season for competitive rodeo runs from spring through fall. The traditional peak time for the largest number of rodeos is the Fourth of July weekend. The modern professional rodeo circuit runs longer, and concludes with the Professional Rodeo Cowboys Association (PRCA) Wranglers National Finals Rodeo (NFR) in Las Vegas, Nevada, which is now held in December. PRCA has a web site with advertisements and a blog for schedules, results, and standings. But it is not a social network.

There are a handful of different events, some for women and others for men.

Timed Events

- Barrel racing and pole bending—the timed speed and agility events seen in rodeo as well as gymkhana or O-Mok-See competition. Both men and women compete in speed events at gymkhanas or O-Mok-Sees; however, at rodeos, barrel racing is an exclusively women's sport. In a barrel race, horse and rider gallop around a cloverleaf pattern of barrels, making agile turns without knocking the barrels over. In pole bending, horse and rider run the length of a line of six upright poles, turn sharply and weave through the poles, turn again and weave back, then return to the start. Only barrel racing is seen in professional competition.

- Steer wrestling—Also known as "bulldogging," this is a rodeo event where the rider jumps off his horse onto a steer and wrestles it to the ground by grabbing it by the horns. This is probably the single most physically dangerous event in rodeo for the cowboy, who runs a high risk of jumping off a running horse head first and missing the steer, or having the thrown steer land on top of him, sometimes horns first.

- Goat tying—usually an event for women or pre-teen girls and boys; a goat is staked out while a mounted rider runs to the goat, dismounts, grabs the goat, throws it to the ground and ties it in the same manner as a calf. This event was designed to teach smaller or younger riders the basics of calf roping without the more complex skill of roping the animal. This event is not part of professional rodeo competition.

Roping

Roping encompasses a number of timed events that are based on the real-life tasks of working cowboys, who often had to capture calves and adult cattle for branding, medical treatment, and other purposes. A lasso or lariat is thrown over the head of a calf or the horns and heels of adult cattle, and the animal is secured in a fashion determined by its size and age.

- Calf roping: A calf is roped around the neck by a lariat; the horse stops and pulls back on the rope while the cowboy dismounts, runs to the calf, throws it to the ground and ties three feet together. (If the horse throws the calf, the cowboy must lose time waiting for the calf to get back to its feet so that the

cowboy can do the work. The job of the horse is to hold the calf steady on the rope.)
- Team roping, also called "heading and heeling," is the only rodeo event where men and women riders may compete together. Two people capture and restrain a full-grown steer. One horse and rider, the "header," lassos a running steer's horns, while the other horse and rider, the "heeler," lassos the steer's two hind legs. Once the animal is captured, the riders face each other and lightly pull the steer between them, so that it loses its balance and lies over, thus, in the real world, allowing restraint for treatment.
- Breakaway roping—an easier form of calf roping where a very short lariat is used, tied lightly to the saddle horn with string and a flag. When the calf is roped, the horse stops, allowing the calf to run on, flagging the end of time when the string and flag breaks from the saddle. In the United States, this event is primarily for women of all ages and boys under 12, while in some nations where traditional "tie-down" calf roping is frowned upon, riders of both genders compete.

Riding

- Bronc riding—There are two divisions in rodeo, bareback bronc riding, where the rider is allowed to hang onto a bucking horse only with a type of surcingle called a "rigging," and saddle bronc riding, where the rider is allowed a specialized western saddle without a horn (or safety) and may hang onto a heavy lead rope, called a bronc rein, which is attached to a halter on the horse.
- Bull riding—an event where the cowboys ride full-grown bulls instead of horses. Although skills and equipment similar to those needed for bareback bronc riding are required, the event differs considerably from horse riding competition due to the danger involved. Because bulls are unpredictable and may

attack a fallen rider, rodeo clowns, now known as *bullfighters*, work during bull riding competition to help prevent injury to the competitors.

Hundreds of millions of people attend rodeos annually. The cowboys and cowgirls travel to attend the events. Yet the rodeo market does not have a rodeoing community magazine or meaningful web presence. The Alexa rating of www.prca.com is 6,520,477. According to compete.com, prca.com had only 1,251 unique visitors in June 2008. The recreational sports community, Sportsvite.com, on the other hand, had 69,371 unique visitors that same month.

This opportunity is big enough to drive a Mack truck through it. Communities can be created for the riders, in which events are listed with dates and prize money; leaderboards; statistics; money leaders; forums; classified ads where the riders trade saddles, boots, hats, and so on; newsletters and a rating, reviewing, and recommending service for the products involved; and the venues. Three online communities could be launched at once: cowboys, cowgirls, and teens. Three more could be launched in the Spanish language.

A fourth could be launched for rodeo fans, with a product sales section, travel pages and sponsorships paid for by RV marketers, pickup truck producers, and chewing tobacco marketers.

Business Plan for Rodeochicks.com

The business plan for a cowgirls online community can be pretty much rubber-stamped to produce a cowboys' online community. The utility of both communities is the following:

Schedule of events
Prize money of events
Statistics, leaderboard

Money standings
Forum—conversation between members
Classified ads: buying and selling used gear
General news contributed by members
Fan mail
Uploading photos and videos of riders and fans at the rodeos
and tailgate parties

Rodeos are heavily attended sporting events. They have a huge fan base of 100 million attendees in 2007 throughout North America. Just shy of 2 million people attended the 2008 Houston Livestock Show and Rodeo. This is just one of dozens of annual rodeos. For rodeochicks.com to succeed, it will have to bring in many fans. The fans will join because they will be able to interact with the cowgirls; so the community will have to be free to the cowgirls also. Where will the revenues come from?

First, there will be "Powered by . . ." sponsors. Many of the fans of rodeos are farmers and ranchers, and they drive pickup trucks. The founders of rodeochicks.com should put Chevrolet, Toyota, Dodge, and Ford in a competition, with the highest bidder receiving a one-year "Powered by . . ." sponsorship. Rodeo is also a photographic event; thus, another "Powered by . . ." link can be auctioned to Kodak, Canon, or Fuji. A third slot could be posted as a request for quotes (RFQ) to the jeans companies—Levi-Strauss, Wrangler, Jordache, and so on. And tennis shoes, belts, Stetsons, lariats, sombreros, and string ties can fill the other slots.

Videos of tailgate parties and outdoor barbecues in the parking lots before and after the rodeos, videos and digital photos of the fans at the events, and videos of the cowgirls doing barrel racing, calf roping, and the other events will become some of the most compelling reasons to visit and join rodeochicks.com. Remember Roger Horchow's mantra: "Put someone's name or initials on a gift and they won't return it to the vendor." The same applies to videos and digital photos: Tell someone you saw her picture on rodeochicks.com, and she will quickly go to the social network and scroll and click around it until she finds her picture. Many of them will find the community very engaging and will join. I see a tip jar page for best photos and best videos.

I know from providing some of the angel capital that launched iboats.com, a leading online boat and boating accessories retailer, that boaters have a lot of used stuff they like to sell to other boaters and that the classified ads business has created profitable pages at iboats. My assumption is that rodeo riders and their fans have lots of stuff to trade as well, and rodeochicks.com could be an easy way to do it; rodeochicks.com will make its money by charging a placement fee for the classified ads rather than slicing off a commission on each sale.

Finally, once the community grows to 30,000 members or so, the homogeneous population of the community—southwestern and western people who like to see young women ride horses and fly off their horses to rope calves—represents an interesting market in which to test a whole bunch of products. These include clothing, boots, cars, trucks, tractors, bush hogs, house paints, barbecues, steak sauce, beer (certainly not wine), rifles, hunting gear, and sporting goods.

The operating expenses are going to be pretty much the same as those we did for creditefficiencies.com in Chapter 1. Exhibit 4.2 shows what the first 12 months' cash flow statement is likely to look like.

Rodeochicks.com begins to break even in the fourth quarter, and as membership continues its steady march northward, it probably will remain in positive cash flow territory by the end of the fifth quarter. In the sponsorship revenue channel, I have included: (1) infomercials and (2) studies for sponsors on the communities'

EXHIBIT 4.2 12-month Cash Flow Projections for Rodeochicks.com

($000s)

	Mo. 1	Mo. 2	Mo. 3	Mo. 4	Mo. 5	Mo. 6	Mo. 7	Mo. 8	Mo. 9	Mo. 10	Mo. 11	Mo. 12	Total Yr. 1
Members	-	-	-	2,500	5,000	7,500	12,500	17,500	22,500	27,500	32,500	37,500	37,500
Revenues:													
Sponsorships	-	30	40	50	60	75	60	80	100	120	150	-	765
Tip Jar	-	-	-	-	-	5	5	5	10	10	10	15	60
Classifieds	-	-	-	-	1	2	3	4	5	6	7	18	36
Product Rating	-	-	-	-	-	-	-	-	40	50	60	100	225
Total Revenues	-	30	40	50	61	82	68	89	155	186	227	143	1,131
Optg. Expenses:													
Systems Engs.[a]	7	7	7	14	14	21	28	35	35	35	42	42	287
Newsletter Pubs.[b]	-	21	21	42	42	42	84	84	84	84	84	84	672
Marketing, Mgmt.[c]	-	12	12	24	24	24	36	36	36	36	36	36	312
Purchase Servers	-	11	-	5	-	-	5	-	-	5	-	10	36
Travel, Telecom	2	3	4	5	6	7	8	9	10	11	12	13	90
Office Rent, Misc.	5	5	5	5	5	5	5	5	5	5	5	5	60
Professional	20	-	-	5	-	-	-	-	-	-	-	10	35
Unspecified	10	10	2	2	2	2	2	5	5	5	5	10	60
Total Optg. Expenses	44	68	78	73	92	93	118	163	174	96	206	192	1,552
Net Optg. Income	(44)	(38)	(38)	(23)	(31)	(11)	(50)	(74)	(19)	6	21	59	(421)

[a] There is one systems engineer for every four servers for every 20,000 members. A systems engineer is paid $72,000 a year plus benefits at 20 percent.

[b] There are initially three employees who gather data for the newsletter, doubling every 12 months, and paid the same as systems engineers. They also produce the reports.

[c] The founder and a marketing team run the Company at a cost of $10,000 per person/mo. plus benefits at 20 percent.

favorite trucks, barbecue sauce, and jeans. These are profitable reports, and the cost of goods sold is basic: slice and dice the conversations, anonymize them, package them into reports, and sell them to the appropriate vendors.

Once you have launched rodeochicks.com, you can segue directly into the social network for the cowboys. Note how quickly you can make things happen for online community number two that you struggled with for number one. For instance, finding the Vice Presidents for Digital Media who handle the four different pickup truck manufacturers, scheduling appointments with them (and/or their advertising agencies), and then selling them on the notion of buying a "Powered by . . ." sponsorship for the home page of an online community in start-up mode, takes some time, costs some money for travel and lodging, and requires some sizable *cojones* to make the sale. I have seen it done: Bruce Failing sold a new medium—mini-billboards on supermarket shopping carts before he had the supermarkets sold on the concept when he launched ActMedia—and lived to see his company acquired by News Corp. for $650 million. My angel fund's capital gain on ActMedia was sumptuous. The gutsy Bruce Failing now runs Alerion Partners, a venture capital fund specializing in supply chain and logistics companies.

The second and third time around will take more phone calls to the sponsors of rodeochicks.com, and if they have been pleased with their online community experience in the first rodeo community, they will surely step up to the plate for the second one.

The infomercial revenue channel virtually screams out to be used in rodeochicks.com and its male and teen copies. People love to watch rodeo, and as you will recall from Chapter 1, there are always some saleable minutes on the ten o'clock evening news—between sports and weather—where digital videos of recent rodeos can be uploaded and paid for by the "Powered by . . ." sponsors. The owners of the communities will earn the ad agency fee of 15 percent. To lay a strong foundation and to tweak the four beginning revenue channels may be enough of a management challenge for rodeochicks.com in year one. But I added it in the fourth quarter to give revenues a pop.

Other Huge Opportunities

A series of online communities are sitting there waiting for bold entrepreneurs to step forward and launch multiples. Exhibit 4.3 shows some ideas.

Purchasing Lagging Communities

Many social networks that have received venture capital are laggards. Their business models have been advertising-based, and as advertisers realize that no one is paying attention, they pull out. The venture capitalists would like to sell these losers, and happily they don't need to sell for cash. If they sold for cash, they would receive far less than they invested, and would be forced to take a writedown.

Writedowns in the world of venture capital are charged against the 20 percent of the capital gains that are awarded to the general partners—the managers—of venture capital funds. Thus, if the venture capital fund with $5 million that is invested in a social network flop writes it down to $1 million, the general partners eat the $4 million loss. If their fund had capital gains of $10 million in the year of the social network loss, they would have to pay out of their pockets $2 million; that is:

$10 million gain $\times$ 20% = $2 million − ($4 million) = ($2 million)

EXHIBIT 4.3   Ideas for Online Communities

Softball	Women Men Teens
Judging Judges	U.S. District Courts State District Courts U.S. Bankruptcy Courts Magistrate Courts
High School Athletics	To give college coaches more information about female athletes, male athletes.
Inventors	Conversations about the U.S. Patent and Trademark office; patent lawyers; changes in laws, etc. Several communities based on fields of interest: medicine; consumer products; software; capital goods.
Automobile Design	Detroit needs recommender online communities to sprout up and aid them in designing cars that the public wants and needs.
Lexicographers	A community for wordsmiths and book editors.
Authors of Children's Books	It is very difficult to launch oneself into the field of writing children's books.
Photographers	A community is needed for photographers to collaborate and post their pictures, so that journal publishers can purchase them. The domain name www.paparazzisunited.com is available. Someone grab it.
Psychotherapists	The sermo.com model could work for this branch of medicine.
Classical Musicians	After launching this community for musicians to solve their pain of needing to collaborate, bifurcate it into strings, brass, woodwinds, and drums.

EXHIBIT 4.3 (*Continued*)

Alternative Medicine	Copy the sermo.com model for acupuncturists and then do several spin-offs: Ayurveda, environmental medicine, homeopathic medicine, Latin American practices, natural products, naturopathic medicine, past-life therapy, Tibetan medicine, and traditional Chinese medicine.
Do-it-Yourself Home	This opportunity desperately needs a community for remodelers, and it can be balkanized into plumbing, carpentry, cement work, stone wall building, roofing, electrical work, and kitchens. The product rate, review, and recommend revenue channel would succeed in this social network.

To avoid that painful event, the venture capital fund with the social network loser will trade stock in their community for a smidgin of stock in your successful community. They will convince their auditors that a 2 percent ownership in your winner is better than, or at least equal to, the $5 million it invested in the social network loser. A win-win all the way around.

5

Loyalty and Passion Builders

LET'S PUT ALL THE CARDS FACE UP, as my grandfather would say. No secrets. No hidden cards. The members create most of the value of online communities, and they are entitled to compensation. Of course, some communities are set up to reward certain of their members who sell their crafts to other members (such as etsy.com), or their tee shirt designs (such as threadless.com); but there are no communities that have a payment system for all of their members (except, of course, the ubiquitous and five-days-to-a-liquidity-event called eBay)—what a brilliant business model is Pierre Omidyar's giant online swap meet.

Mechanisms for Rewarding Members

The Securities and Exchange Commission (SEC), a policing agency dedicated to preventing unscrupulous people from selling crappy securities to widows and orphans, as well as the unsophisticated investor; plus practically every state's securities regulatory commission, has regulations that will prohibit you, the founder, of an online community, from selling stock in your community to its members. It is not a good idea to do it.

97

But, you protest, you want to make 20 percent of your community's stock available to your members at a steep discount from the price paid by angel investors. Let's say the angels paid $1 per share and they bought 500,0000 shares for $500,000. Your founders and early employees own 2,000,000 shares, and you want to issue 600,000 shares to the first 10,000 members, in units of 60 shares per member for a payment of $6.00 (10 cents per share).

The first problem with this is that the members will incur taxable events of $54.00 per person. While not large, they will owe an income tax of roughly one-third of that amount.

Second, a small number of shares would require registration with the state securities commission of every state in which the members live. These state laws, known as "blue sky" laws, are expensive to comply with. As a start-up, your community's shares will not pass muster in Florida, Pennsylvania, and several other states with highly restrictive blue sky laws.

Third, you could be making yourself a publicly traded company, because you will have way too many stockholders. The SEC may force you to file a registration statement and have your stock trading on the bulletin board or pink sheets, which is for companies that are too small or do not audit their financial statements, and thus have "Beware" written all over them. Being publicly traded as a start-up is a very bad idea, requiring audited financial statements and compliance with Sarbanes Oxley, which generally costs more than $200,000 a year; and finally, your competitors will learn a lot about your operations by reading your public filings.

Therefore, as good-hearted as your intentions may be, you may have to come up with other loyalty builders.

Pretty much everything I discuss in this chapter you learned in kindergarten or summer camp, or playing Red Rover with your neighborhood friends when you were a child. Although I call the chapter by its business name—*loyalty builders*—what that means is "glue." Think back to those sunny, languid summer days when you were six or seven or eight, and ask yourself, "What made me keep coming to the backyard with no idea of what the day's activities or events would be?" What made you laugh? What held your interest? Was it discovery? Maybe it was adopting nicknames for everyone in the group—Gonger, Boogers, Goose, Pigeon Chest, Teeters—these were some that I recall from sunny Knoxville summers when I was a child—or ranking—Gonger climbed highest into the magnolia tree—or building something together like a rickety wheelbarrow and carrying Pigeon Chest and Boogers in it around the yard, with the dogs barking and jumping in circles. The happy and rewarding things that made us return over and over again are the things that will make your members return over and over again to your community.

I will list them, and then we will peel back the onion and discuss why they work; I will create a hypothetical online community and apply the loyalty builders:

- Mapping or "watch us grow"
- Every member gets her own web site
- Every member gets a membership identifier, a hat, a tee shirt, or a loyalty debit card
- Members are searchable by victories
- Lockers
- Closets
- Award status, with the goal of reaching "elite"
- Enterpreneurship Is Gift Giving
- Spokesperson
- The unexpected rewards

Mapping or "Watch Us Grow"

Your web page will need to have a map icon that opens to a page called "Watch us Grow." When a member clicks onto "Watch Us Grow," she can see how many members have joined the community that week, or that month, in her region. The region could be the state she lives in or the country. It could be the region she lives in, such as the Northeast or Eastern Europe. One of the ways a member can gain "elite" status is by recruiting new members. Points will be awarded to members, and stored in their closets along with a number of achievements—one is new members she recruited and another is exceptional reporting on the good things done by the industrial companies being rated and reviewed by the community. Yet another is unexpected and unique contributions to the community, such as outing a wolf in sheep's clothing or convincing a celebrity spokesperson to become a member and raising awareness of the community when he or she is interviewed, for instance, on Larry King's television show.

The map needs to be designed with specificity as to the states or regions that the community members determine as important in measuring growth and their contribution to membership growth. For instance, if the members, in their collective wisdom, believe that the ubiquity of the Web makes state-by-state growth meaningless and they prefer regional membership growth as a more inclusive means of recording growth and giving out awards to members for bringing in more members, then the "Watch Us Grow" page should forget about listing Arkansas, Texas, Oklahoma, and Louisiana specifically, and just group all of these states into one large region called Southwest. But if your online community, for instance, is designed to bring high school football players and their achievements to the attention of Division 1 college football coaches, then your "Watch Us Grow" page should be more granular than state by state. For instance, for high school football players in Tennessee, the map would have to break out Bristol, Kingsport, Knoxville, Chattanooga, Nashville, and Memphis as well as regions in between these dominant cities, such as Jackson and the space between Knoxville and Chattanooga, which could be Cleveland. If your community is international and devoted to environmental biodiversity in Latin America and saving the forests for the species that dwell in them while preventing loggers and developers from hacking down the forests, the "Watch Us Grow" page has to show membership growth country by country because biodiversity is an international challenge.

And remember, maximize design and minimize words. A map is a map. Everyone knows the shape of their state and their country. What will interest them the most is the accuracy of the headcount and watching it click, like the electronic clock near Penn Station in New York City, which records the dollar size of the national debt annually and minute-by-minute.

Every Member Has Her Own Web Site

Each member will be given a web site on your community's portal. On our personal web sites we will provide information about ourselves to the extent we wish. Let's take the example of an online community for collectors of antique cars. Among the things important to this community would be the kinds of cars you collect, regional events where collectors meet and show off their cars, and of course the brokers and dealers who facilitate purchases and sales. They will be rated, reviewed, and recommended, but first the community has to be built. Lets call this community "myantiquecar.com."

Upon joining myantiquecar.com, the members will be given a web site and they will list their avatar name or their pseudonym, the kinds of cars they collect, photographs and other information about their cars, and their reasons for joining the community. The latter could be "I want to buy more classic Jaguars from the 1960s" or "I want to meet other collectors who share my passion for Morgans," or for older collectors, "My kids don't want my old MGs and I will be selling them pretty soon."

You will need a web site designer or perhaps several of them to work with new members to design their web sites. Some of the new members may not have digital cameras with which to photograph their cars, and that will require the community owner arranging a strategic alliance with Fujitsu or Kodak to solve that problem. A finders fee to the community for initiating the sale and, equally important, hands-on training through the partner's customer service department would be appropriate. When we get to the loyalty builder called "The Unexpected Rewards," we will discuss how corporate sponsors will be asked to pay for these surprise rewards to members.

The Membership Identifier

Upon joining the community, the new member will receive a membership identifier. You're probably thinking tee shirts or coffee mugs, but that's so yesterday. You will want something appropriate to the mission of your community that at the same time makes the new member feel that she has joined something of importance in her life. The Lance Armstrong wristband still has legs. Hystersisters.com uses a wristband as a loyalty builder. The site wristbandconnection.com offers 75 varieties in different colors that are preprinted with the name of your community. The wristband is appropriate for communities whose members get out and mix with their fellow citizens in offline communities such as churches, the Kiwanis Club, scrapbook and book clubs, and local beekeepers' groups.

Other identifiers include branded flash drives, branded Post-its, a subscription to *Wired* magazine, bumper stickers, mousepads, and my favorite, the loyalty prepaid credit card. This is a card that is issued by a community or club with the name of the community on it, and endorsed by Visa or MasterCard, that will use one of its banks to clear the purchases and share a portion of the $3.50 per purchase fee with the community that issues the loyalty card. Typically, the community earns $1.00 of the $3.50. As the loyalty card is used to make offline purchases, people can see the name of the community on the card and perhaps get into a conversation with the cardholder and then join the community.

An online community that helps teenagers learn financial conservatism and responsible buying habits, while at the same time providing them with a prepaid credit card for online and offline purchases, is UPsidecard.com, owned by Plastyc, Inc. This community goes one step further and brands the UPsidecard for groups of teenagers who are members of online and offline communities gathered by their high school into bands, or cheerleaders, or gathered by camp owners or colleges. It is the myriad uses of the prepaid credit card that makes it the most interesting and centripetal loyalty identifier. A branded bobble-head does not have the revenue-generating capability of the branded prepaid credit card; nor does the wristband. The community can wire-transfer unexpected rewards and other payments to a member who is issued a loyalty card. A member with a loyalty card can make purchases on the community or pay his monthly reputation management fee with the card. Members can be paid tip jar payments directly into their loyalty cards if the community endorses that revenue channel.

You might consider multiple membership identifiers. Remember the sunny summer days with your playmates, when you created secret clubs and only the playmates with the password could enter the club's treehouse or secret hiding place? There was often more than one password, or sometimes you had to perform a special feat, like having to capture a lightning bug and a tadpole, *and* know the secret entrance word. The same applies in creating glue among the members of your community. You could begin with a prepaid credit card and then have a store in the community to enable club members to buy additional identifiers, such as baseball caps, wristbands, and bumper stickers.

Baseball cards have been popular with young and old alike for 150 years. Why not send members a trading card with their face on it, and their membership info on the back? Multiple member cards can be collected for kudos points and traded. Those with the most extensive collection can be paid an unexpected reward.

Baseball cards were initially ancillary to major league baseball, but when Marvin Miller became head of the players union, he negotiated vigorously with the CEO of Topps, the leading baseball card producer. Soon, players who were receiving $120 from Topps to use their image were getting $8,000. The value and importance of trading cards to show one's loyalty to a team was always there, and still is there. Their popularity has extended to all sports at all levels and into the field of music. They have a certain magic and should be considered by many kinds of communities.

Members Are Searchable by Victories

Your members will want to be known by their accomplishments on behalf of the community. Let's say the community you form rates, reviews, and recommends Native American basketry and their dealers. From time to time, fraudulent items enter the market, and one of the main purposes of the community—let's call it basketrylovers.com—is to help members spot frauds and the perpetrators of frauds. At the same time, it operates a forum for the discussion of baskets, a market for the buying and selling of baskets, and a daily index that shows prices by regions, state, and country. Native American baskets go up steadily in price, with the setbacks primarily in deep recessions and when there is a fraud scare.

Thus, it is to everyone's best interest in the community, because they are likely to be collectors, to tar and feather the fraudulent basket dealers, and to encourage others to join to begin collecting baskets. Merchants of baskets will be charged subscription fees, and collectors will be admitted for free.

You will want to put an icon on the home page of basketry-lovers.com called "Victories." When a member clicks on Victories, he will open a page that cites the achievements of members who spotted fraudulent Native American baskets, such as copies made in Zimbabwe selling for 1 percent of the price of a fine Zuni fetish basket, and then passed off as Zuni at collectors shows in Flagstaff, Arizona. A member will also be given victory points for spotting baskets that come onto the market from gravediggers. A member will gain victory points for spotting baskets that someone attempts to sell in the community that have sacred objects on them, and thus belong to a tribe and not to private collectors. Victory points can also be awarded for outstanding photographs, for the particular beauty of a member's collection as voted on by the community, and for bringing in 50 new members. It may sound corny that a bunch of middle-aged people who buy Native American baskets for investments and artistic purposes would get their jollies from seeing their name in the Victories section of basketrylovers.com's web portal, but everyone loves recognition, and recognition among a group of people who share a particular interest is the best recognition of all.

Milton Friedman used to say, jokingly perhaps, that when an economist is asked to compliment the work of a fellow economist, he will usually say, "Charlie plays a terrific game of bridge." In other words, extending a pat on the back, a "hip, hip, hooray," and an "attaboy" is not done enough. But it is done beautifully in multilevel marketing companies. These selling machines have gotten a lot of bad press because of some of their naughty techniques, such as forcing new sales recruits to purchase a kit of sales tools for $250, when the multilevel marketing company knows that 90 percent of all recruits last two weeks on average. But MLM organizations (that's their moniker) have introduced some exceptional loyalty-building features. I have attended several of their national sales meetings at which trophies and "attaboys" are handed out, and they capture the fervor of a Super Bowl game. The CEO has a script, and he describes the background of the people he will soon call up to the dais, and to say the script is effectively written would be an understatement.

Here's how it works: Nobody knows who the winners are, and the CEO and several young ladies from the sales department stand on the dais announcing the achievements for the most sales for the year, most sales in a region, most sales by a first-year salesperson, and so forth. The winners run up to the front to stupendous applause, fist-pumping and high-fiving other sales people along the way, and when they reach the front, they do a Rocky-style victory dance, shake the CEO's hand, clutch their trophy, and receive kisses on the cheek from the young ladies. They then high-five their way to the back of the room to more applause, hoots, and hollers. These are grown-ups, mind you. Winners of these sales awards who have suffered earlier defeats in their lives, or overcome addiction, or lost a leg in a car crash, not only receive all of the above forms of adulation and war whoops, but there isn't a dry eye in the place. Talk about glue! The victory page of your community's web portal should be equally a combination of Friday night at a Texas high school football game and schmaltz, and the award ceremony should be used at the annual users group meeting. It is extraordinarily powerful and has a religious base, which brings us back to bread and pastry. Don't forget to serve celebratory cake at these events and have the top achiever cut the first slice.

Lockers

The inimitable comedian George Carlin, who left us mortals to entertain God in June 2008, used to do a very funny routine about his "stuff." He never defined what his "stuff" was exactly, but by innuendo we learned that it was his things. His collections. Is that clear?

In an online community we need a place to store our stuff. We will accumulate things, such as passwords, addresses, kudos, favorite videos, loyalty builders, songs that have a personal meaning, avatar outfits, synthetic currency, old newsletters, special e-mails, perhaps congratulating us on a story, and well, you know, things. These are personal. These are ours.

Community builders, take note. Your members will want some personal space, a private storage area that no one else is entitled to enter. It's the *locker*.

This is a digression. When a community member dies, can a family member with a copy of grandpa's death certificate clean out his locker? The answer is *no*, not unless he left specific instructions in his will that his heirs were entitled to his password and the contents of his locker and anything else that were his assets in the community, according to the terms and conditions. So a note to the one or two Wills and Estates lawyers who may be reading this book, there is a new revenue channel for you adding language to the wills and estate plans of your boomer clients to the following effect: "And to my darling grandchildren, I leave my password 'bucolic68' on the following communities, to do with it as they wish: www.mycoincollection.com, www.mycolonialcurrencycollection.com, and www.myantiquejaguars.com."

Randy Farmer, a brilliant community maven who ran five of Yahoo's online communities for many years, told me the story of a family who fought like the dickens to gain access to their father's passwords, thus to capture information about his assets and passions, but to no avail. In just about every community with which I have come in contact, the terms and conditions provide that the community owners/operators will guard the member's locker contents with a moat around it and angry pit bulls standing sentinel at the drawbridge.

Some of you will be building social networks that are concerned with assets such as stamp and coin collections, investments, real estate, currencies, art, and antiques. This will be the case as younger boomers with greater computer literacy than the first crop become builders of online communities. Be sure your members write that they "gift my password on the following communities to Jane, Robert, and Irving, my beloved grandchildren" into their wills.

Of course, if you are looking for a new online community to start, why not become the owner of passwordformyheirs.com, a collection place for everyone who joins a community and has a user name and password for each one to safely store his or her password in one location. Thus, you take away a revenue channel from the Wills and Estates lawyers by offering an archiving and storage service. The fee could be $25 a year, or, to generate cash up front, offer an alternative: $350 payable upfront and no payments later on.

Your community's name and mission statement can then be sent via e-mail and regular mail to every lawyer in the country, and in foreign countries, who lists himself as having a Wills and Estates practice. He will recommend passwordsformyheirs.com whenever he draws up a will. You can search engine optimize (SEO) it on Google and the other search engines to bring in more revenues. This idea will make you money while you sleep.

Closets

Closets are lockers, but they don't contain any secrets. Closets are where members store things that they wish to share with other members. These include their points for bringing in new members, their tip jar winnings, their schedule for participating in an online focus group to assist Kimberly Clark in creating a Kleenex product for keeping the terminal and keyboard clean, or for participating in several upcoming votes on a new infant car seat that Honda intends to add in its 2010 hydrogen-fueled mommy car. With all the rating, reviewing, ranking, recommending, and new products branding that community members will increasingly be asked to do, the closet will be a busy storage unit. And you want it to be busy. It is a glue factor.

Award Status with the Potential of Earning Elite Status

We can look to the various religious orders for guidance in creating a hierarchy within the communities. Our role as builders/maintainers of the communities will be to monitor and shape the conversations, but we will early on set up an award system to encourage our members to stay glued to the community for an increasing number of hours per week. To do that, awards will be given for (1) bringing in new members by the truckload, (2) participating in all of the product and service branding and testing requests that are brought into the community, (3) a perfect or near-perfect attendance record at physical user group meetings, (4) storytelling contests where the stories involve working with other members for some common good, (5) introducing strategic partners that spend money at the community, (6) getting publicity for the community on Oprah's TV show, the *Today* show, or *Good Morning America*.

People love to be recognized for their contributions, and pity the community owner/operator who fails to recognize a member's efforts. The strata of awards might begin at bronze, then work their way up to silver, then gold-elite, the highest rank.

What does it mean? It means what you want it to mean. Study some of the old business books on party-plan selling or multi-level marketing, or the sales strategies of products that *have to be sold*, because nobody would buy them unless a skilled salesperson had trained them, such as annuities, mutual funds, life insurance, extended care insurance, and face-amount certificates like those sold by Ameriprise. These sales training manuals are filled with tactics for creating the glue.

There is a difference between products that have to be sold and products that have to be bought. Annuities have to be sold; life insurance has to be sold; investments by angels in online communities have to be sold. And memberships in social networks have to be sold.

Milk, orange juice, clothes, cars, kitchen utensils, linens, towels, diapers (if you are a young parent), hearing aids (if you're hearing impaired), automobile insurance, and many other products and services that we use in our daily lives have to be bought.

You must have the steel will of a salesperson to be an owner-operator of an online community. If you are more the creative type of person who likes to create an image for a product that differentiates it from other have-to-be-bought products, then you might not be successful at owning and operating a social network.

Entrepreneurship Is Gift Giving

Entrepreneurship is gift giving. Entrepreneurs are society's altruists. When we compete in the marketplace, we are attempting to give gifts of great value to our customers. "Competition is giving," George Gilder writes. "Entrepreneurs [provide] contests of altruism . . . the contest of gifts leads to an expansion of human sympathies. The circle of giving (the profits of the economy) will grow as long as the gifts are consistently valued more by the receivers than the giver."

Entrepreneurs compete with one another to see whose gifts will be perceived as having the greatest value. Entrepreneurs are altruists who achieve great wealth in a land of egotists. The functional role of the entrepreneur in the community is to develop new markets that will create productivity and employment, to solve problems that affect large numbers of people, and to create wealth that will lead to reinvestment and further giving.

Spokesperson

Although you will appoint a monitor from within your management team, you will need some people to provide the functions of early "chatter."

Ewan MacLeod, one of the brightest young social network entrepreneurs in the United Kingdom, who has built and sold a number of businesses based on parties, music, and the mobile phone, recently launched themobileinternetdirectory.com, a blog that reviews, discusses, and rates mobile phones and their new features. Prior to that, he launched NeoOne, a company that started chat groups for large companies. Ewan played all of the roles—questioner, answerer, new voice, and so on. He sold the business at a huge profit. You and your early employees will have to operate NeoOne to lift off your membership drive.

The Unexpected Rewards

The surprise payment of real money to a member will be a conversation piece that will travel quickly, like in the children's game *Whisper*. Then, a second unexpected payment to another member a few months later will get the parishioners sitting on the edge of their chairs. "Payment for what?" you ask. Several things: The most important in the early days is to make a surprise payment to a member who brings in 10 other members. Then do it again for a member who brings in 20 members. Pay a member who gets the community some ink in the important magazines that relate to the topics discussed in your community. Pay a member who blogs about your community. Pay a member who best describes in an essay contest why he or she comes to the community every day. Don't announce what the winner will get, and then wire $500 into his or her account. Report the event in the community newsletter. If you make unexpected rewards four or five times a year, the members will be like Pavlov's dogs, lining up to help the community in one way or another.

Returning to the Concept of Shared Ownership

The egalitarian on my left shoulder says, "Share ownership in the community with members." The securities lawyers on my right shoulder say, "You will regret it." Here is a middle ground.

Successful online communities are currently being valued at very high prices. The online community etsy.com, for artisans and craftspeople, raised $25 million from Accel Partners, a smart venture capital fund, just after a year in which it showed revenues of $1.75 million. Assuming that estsy.com's founder didn't give away control, but rather (this is a guess) 40 percent ownership, the investment valued etsy.com at $62.5 million. That's more than 30 times trailing revenues. *Wow!*

If you may someday sell all or a piece of your community for 30 times trailing revenues, why not send a wire transfer of $1,000 to all of your members when the founders' bank accounts are stuffed with million-dollar bills. The members will be grateful, and perhaps join your next community.

6

Disruption: The Sumptuous Impertinence

You can forget about the sustainability of MySpace, Facebook, and other general-purpose online social networks. They aren't sustainable businesses. Their business model, based on advertising, is not demonstrably economically justifiable. Very few of their members look at the ads, and billions of dollars are being wasted trying to reach them. These social networks will continue to attract younger people who, ironically, lack spending power. Until that day on Madison Ave. when the light bulb is turned on and consumer advertisers realize that they need to find a reliable venue to capture input about their brands, the waste and disconnect will continue. At that time, the force that will suck them away is the *online recommender community* because it serves a real economic purpose for the vendors of consumer products and services that we use every day.

The creation and spread of online recommender communities will be revolutionary in its scope and its effect on the way goods and services are marketed. Except for a few subscription-based industries, where finding a new customer results in a continuum of payments to the vendor, such as insurance, most producers of consumer products and services use an antiquated method that I call the "antelope hunt." It follows the prehistoric model of find the customer (usually through television advertising, but sometimes with door-hangings and direct mail), sell something to the customer, then go out and find another customer. This is a male thing, since many women-owned businesses ask the customer to pay in advance, for the simple reason that women entrepreneurs haven't been able to attract their proportionate share of capital, and thus have relied over the years on customer float. See Mary Kay Cosmetics, Weight Watchers International, and Gymboree for examples. But male-dominated producers of goods and services have relied on their ancestral genes to find the antelope through the hunt: Find it, kill it, bring it back to the family, skin and eat it, and then go out and find another one.

The antelope-hunt model keeps the prices of goods and services higher than necessary because the process of finding the customer is wasteful and costly. In fact, the antelope-hunt model shrinks the market with each sale, whereas the online recommender community business model expands the market with each sale. The growth and expansion of recommender communities will reduce the need to find the customer through advertising, because the members of recommender communities will do the heavy lifting associated with judging new and old consumer brands. By heavy lifting I mean bear most of the costs of sales and marketing that are currently borne by the producers of goods and services. Members locate the community with their time and money, they join and contribute their time and information to the other members, they pay to collaborate about the products and services that are the nucleating force of their particular communities, they pay to attend users group meetings, and ultimately they purchase products voted on by the community. Producers of goods and services will be able to lower prices because their customers will pay for the cost of search. This will result in layoffs of many members of the sales and marketing departments of the big brand companies. And, if the votes of the communities go against certain brands, they could die as well.

Branding

There are more than 14 million people in sales and marketing occupations in the United States, according to the Bureau of Labor Statistics. Many of them will be laid off, and what was spent on them will be converted into wealth earned by entrepreneurs and their backers and employees who launch successful online recommender communities. Procter & Gamble spends approximately $7 billion a year on sales and marketing. Its budget will be slashed to perhaps one-seventh of that amount, because the find-the-consumer process will be taken on by the new communities.

How will online recommender communities make money and become sustainable? The stronger ones will have as many as 18 revenue channels. Those that review, rate, and recommend consumer products and services will earn money through a *nineteenth revenue channel: new product branding*. With television viewing declining, consumer products and service companies are seeking new ways to develop and introduce new brands. Recommender communities will fill the function of brand market testing in the future, and the product and service companies will pay them for it.

Here's how it will work. Let's say that an innovative and energetic entrepreneur launches an online recommender community called agonyairlines.com. People flock to it to tell airline screw-up stories and stories of airline personnel misspeaking, and on the flip side they tell of services well-performed and on-time arrivals. The members will review, rate, and rank the airlines in dozens of categories from junk found in the seat pocket upon boarding, to filthy toilets, and for untruthful statements concerning delayed departure times, in order to hold frustrated passengers in the boarding area and to prevent them from rebooking with a competitive carrier.

We'll say that agonyairlines.com is a free community and that it generates its revenues primarily through the slice-and-dice channel: selling the anonymized conversations of the members to the airlines and the regulators for $10,000 per month. It's booking $200,000 per month in revenues and incurring $35,000 per month in operating expenses, for net operating income of $165,000 per month. Agonyairlines.com is what's known as a cash cow. But, it's just about to get better.

Airline marketing executives begin calling agonyairlines. com and asking the company to test new products and services. Here are some of the queries that agonyairlines.com begins receiving:

Q: Say, we're thinking of offering frequent business flyers the option of paying us a lump sum on January 1 and then they can fly free throughout the year. Could you have this plan reviewed, priced, and branded by your community? What will you charge us?

A: Yes, we can: $100,000 for reviewing, pricing, and branding.

Q: So, could you ask your group if they would like to be handed snacks as they board the planes? What will they charge us?

A: Yes, we can: $75,000 we think is a fair price.

Q: We are at a loss concerning new services to offer our passengers, notwithstanding our title of Director, Strategic Planning, Trans-Ocean Airlines. Do you think your members could provide us with their list of top 10 new ideas for running our airline better? And how much would that cost us?

A: Yes, we would be delighted to handle *your* job for you. We'll charge Trans-Ocean $250,000.

That, I believe, is how new products and services will be introduced in the future. Control will shift to truthful, safe communities; ones in which members' "social assets" are protected.

By that I mean that if Sally speaks freely about her health problems on patientslikeme.com, or another health-care-oriented community—assuming spidering software doesn't somehow sneak into the community, grab Sally's "social assets," and sell them to Big Pharma, Fair Isaac Corp., or predators who see a vulnerable woman—truthful, safe, and trusted social networks will attract many branding and new product contracts and fee income. More money-making ideas are the following:

American Express wants to introduce a pink American Express card to raise money for breast cancer research, with a percentage of every interest charge earned by American Express going to find a cure for breast cancer. It asks hystersisters.com, eco-chick.com, caresquare.com, patientslikeme.com, mix.com, and two or three other communities to vote up or down on the pink card, participate in the design, come up with a slogan, and suggest ideas for maximizing the buzz through the Web as the pink card is launched. The cost to American Express: $60,000 per community, or $600,000. That is the price of a 30-second ad on a prime-time TV show, but rather than using TV and catching a potpourri of viewers, American Express reaches one million or so women who use their time and brains to review, rank, and recommend products and services in health-care communities.

This next example is quite a bit different and very disruptive. Assume that Van Buren Life Insurance Co., a multibillion-dollar, NYSE-listed insurance company, has a dark, dirty secret—it overcharges Hispanic Americans for their life insurance polices. This is an unethical practice but it is too profitable for Van Buren to stop doing it.

But the employees who know about the policy, and who are upset about it, and who want to have the unethical CEO fired for not coming clean about it, have an idea. They place a Van Buren Life Platform in a number of online communities that aggregate insider stories and truth-revealing scoops about corporate and political goofs and screw-ups. These include rethos.com, mix.com, dig.com, and protest.com, among others. Then the disgruntled employees, using noncorporate e-mail addresses, bombard these platforms with stories about the dark side of the Van Buren CEO—all of it factual—until the story is picked up by Bloomberg, CNNMoney, and the *Wall Street Journal*, and the CEO resigns and the Hispanic Americans get their overpayment money refunded.

Think this second scenario can't happen? Even the French, who love to protest by burning tires in congested city intersections, have turned to the Internet to do their protesting.

This story recently appeared in the *Economist*:

Technology is also transforming traditional industrial disputes. Blogs are being used to draw outside attention to disputes within companies and win support from consumers, politicians and the local community. Workers at a subsidiary of FNC, a retailer, used a blog to rally support and gather evidence for a redundancy protest, which they then took to employment tribunals. Workers at a Savoy furniture firm used a blog in a campaign that won them an improved redundancy offer. At La Redoute, another store chain, workers have set up a blog called "On redoute La Redoute" (we fear La Redoute) to stay informed about possible closures of branches and call centers, and organize resistance.

The Internet allows expressions of discontent to be aggregated, giving workers the opportunity to stage protests without actually going on strike. The most dramatic example came last September in Italy, at the local arm of IBM. About 2,000 employees of the computer giant—logging on from home to dodge legal problems—staged a virtual protest against a new pay settlement at IBM's corporate campus in SecondLife, an online virtural world. A month later the head of IBM Italy resigned and the RSU union agreed on a new pay deal. This innovative use of the Internet was recognized with an award at the Forum Netxplorateur, a conference held in Paris in February. The award was presented by the president of Microsoft France.

Schumpeter Predicted the Disruption That Is Coming

Joseph A. Schumpeter (1883–1950), the first economist to describe the role of the entrepreneur in society, said that the entrepreneur has an important role in the world: what he called "creative destruction." We need to recognize Schumpeter for being a stand-up guy for all of us who disrupt and solve pain for a living.

Schumpeter's relationships with the ideas of other economists were quite complex in his most important contributions to economic analysis—the theory of business cycles and development. Schumpeter starts in *The Theory of Economic Development* with a treatise of circular flow, which, excluding any innovations and innovative activities, leads to a stationary state. The stationary state is, according to Schumpeter, described by Walrasian equilibrium, named for the economist, Leon Walras. The hero of his story is not the economist, Walras; it is the entrepreneur, says Schumpeter.

The entrepreneur disturbs this equilibrium and is the cause of economic development, which proceeds in cyclic fashion along several time scales.

So in Schumpeter's theory Walrasian equilibrium is not adequate to capture the key mechanisms of economic development. Schumpeter also thought that the institution enabling the entrepreneur to purchase the resources needed to realize his or her vision was a well-developed capitalist financial system, including a whole range of institutions for granting credit. He virtually predicted the modern venture capital industry.

Creative destroyer. Disrupter. Painsolver. These are the other names for "entrepreneur." You may be called worse, as your recommender online communities change the way in which new and existing products are introduced to the marketplace and sold. Your recommender online community could achieve gatekeeper status in some industries whose pricing and marketing practices have not been very transparent. When that happens, watch fur fly.

Lawyers for traditional industries may try to sue you back to the Stone Age. But your defense will be the truthfulness that you maintain in your recommender social network. Play by the rules, and the bloviating lawyers will have to put away their cannons.

Voting Communities

It's not just health-care concerns where the wisdom of crowds is being used to make money (although effective treatments for serious illnesses are the most searched-for information in online communities), but it is also in apparel that online communities can show their stuff. CollarFree, an online community that attracts apparel designers and members who want to wear clothing that their peers think is terrific, provides a marketplace for designers and consumers.

The designers present digital photos of their goods, and the community votes. CollarFree then produces and sells back to the members the winning items, and it sells them through boutiques as well. Its revenues are reported to be around $500,000 a year in their first full year of operations, and growing like a rocket. At iboats.com, an online community for boaters, there are 230,000 searches for information about boats and boating accessories every month, which are answered by 1,100,000 members, according to Bruno Vassell III, iboat.com's cofounder and chairman. Fast-growing communities are those that review, rate, and recommend wine; home furniture based on its "greenness," neighborhoods, teeth whiteners and oral hygiene, and corporations based on their compensation and sales commission rates, as well as the truthfulness of their ads and the competitiveness of their products. Coming along more slowly are communities focused on good citizenship, which review, rate, and report on political promises made during election years, and what the politicians actually do after they are elected.

Move over, Tupperware. The EcoMom party has arrived, as reported in the *New York Times*, with its ever-expanding to-do list that includes preparing waste-free school lunches; lobbying for green building codes; transforming oneself into a "locavore," eating locally grown food; and remembering not to idle the car when picking up children from school (if one must drive). Here, the smalltalk is about the volatile compounds emitted by dry-erase markers at school.

Perhaps not since the days of dishpan hands has the household been so all-consuming. But instead of gleaming floors and sparkling dishes, the obsession is with installing compact fluorescent light bulbs, buying in bulk, and using smart power strips that shut off electricity to the espresso machine, microwave, X-Boxes, televisions, and laptops when not in use.

"It's like eating too many brownies one day and then jogging extra the next," said Kimberly Danek Pinkson, 38, the founder of the EcoMom Alliance, speaking to the group of efforts to curb eco-guilt through carbon offsets for air travel.

Part "Hints from Heloise" and part political self-help group, the alliance, which Ms. Pinkson says has 9,000 members across the country, joins a growing subculture dedicated to the green mom, with blogs and web sites like greenandcleanmom.blogspot.com and eco-chick.com. Web-based organizations like the Center for a New American Dream in Takoma Park, Maryland, advocate reducing consumption and offer a registry that helps brides "celebrate the less-material wedding of your dreams."

At an EcoMom circle in Palo Alto, executive mothers whipped out spreadsheets to tally their goals, inspired by a two-step program that urges using only nontoxic products for cleaning, bathing, and make up, as well as cutting down garbage by 10 percent.

"I used to feel anxiety," said Kathy Miller, 49, an alliance member, recalling life before she started investigating weather-sensitive irrigation controls for her garden with nine growing zones. "Now I feel I'm doing something."

Marketplace power is shifting to consumers who join online recommender communities and thus gain *oligopsony* power. The power will shake the owners of major brands to their roots, and some of them will rattle their legal sabers to no avail, except to heighten the awareness of and build the strength of the communities. But, in time, new brands will be tested in the communities, and members' anonymized conversations concerning the products and services will be sliced, diced, and sold back to the consumer products and services producers, and that will put the nail in the coffin of the antelope-hunt business model. Before the light of day registers with the consumer giants, "there will be a new kind of grief," as Saul Bellow wrote in *Mr. Sammler's Planet*. Recommender community entrepreneurs will disrupt the way goods and services have been marketed with a stealth force akin to that of the Navy Seals.

The online community and mobile social network model is elegant and brings people together like the old watercooler days, but the principal reason why communities and networks will thrive is that they *expand the market with each sale*. By this I mean that the customer finds the online community or mobile social network of his or her choice, and then pays a monthly fee for the privilege of contributing knowledge and sharing searches and information with people who share a similar pain and are seeking solutions for it. The customer is locked in for a year or longer, depending on the length of his or her subscription agreement.

The Endowment Effect

And if someone owns something, such as a membership in a recommender community, she values it very highly. Economist and sports collectibles trader John List proved this at sports card trading conventions where he offered premium prices to try to persuade people to sell their cards to him. He wrote, "People suddenly value objects more highly simply because they own them. They won't trade even when the logic suggests they should. Economists call this "the endowment effect." (*see* John A. List, "Does Market Experience Eliminate Anomalies," *Quarterly Journal of Economics* [February 2003].)

A new subscription customer doesn't have to be found with costly advertising. He finds the community on his own, by searching for a pain-solver to apply to his particular need. Once he has found the community and joined it, the endowment effect binds him to the group.

The endowment effect, discovered by economist Richard Thaler, in a 1980 paper in the *Journal of Economic Behavior*, sometimes referred to as the *divestiture aversion*, is the proposition that people value a good or service more once their property right to it has been established. In other words, people place a higher value on things they own relative to objects they do not. Tim Harford, the brilliant *Financial Times* economist, devotes quite a bit of ink to the endowment effect in his book, *The Logic of Life* (New York: Random House, 2008).

So why haven't the major consumer products and services companies entered the online community business? Because they are not as trustworthy as entrepreneurs. They push their own products and services when they form communities, and that is considered a nontruthful act. None of the major consumer products and services companies commands a very high Alexa rating. On the other hand, the recommender and review site Angieslist.com has an Alexa rating of 22,921 and it had 571,816 unique visitors in June 2008. Angieslist.com rates, reviews, and recommends local service providers such as plumbers and electricians.

The largest sales forces in the United States will drastically shrink in the next five years as the number of recommender communities grows and they become more emboldened by their successes.

In some cases, where acts of corporations are particularly egregious, entire corporations will be shunned as a result of the power of recommender communities. An early example concerns the $2 billion (annual revenues) Diebold Election Systems Corporation, and how the state of Ohio was forced to remove its error-prone voting machines when a call to arms by Bev Harris, using her blog, blackboxvoting.com, spread through the Internet like wildfire. Two students at Swarthmore College collected and redistributed the e-mails concerning Diebold's improprieties, and faced down threats of legal action by Diebold by moving their files through peer-to-peer networks to other students' computers throughout the country in what they called an act of "electronic civil disobedience." They then sued Diebold, "seeking a judicial declaration that their posting of the materials was privileged," and they won their case.

The Diebold comeuppance will be considered by historians, I believe, as the first incident of economic disruption in the Age of Recommender Communities

Pain Solving

The pain solving that will occur over the next several years will be equally tectonic as consumers join truthful marketplaces. It is in marketplaces of complete truthfulness that prices come down to the marginal cost of the product, which pays the worker who made it, and a profit to the entrepreneur who took the risk of making it, but no more. At the major corporations, gross profit margins will collapse by 20 percent to 50 percent, but the corporations will still be profitable because they will no longer spend much of their gross profit on advertising, selling, sales commissions, and marketing costs. Online communities and mobile social networks will do their marketing for them. But it will be marketing with a twist. My compass shows me that one of the biggest twists is this: If the vendors of goods and services do not meet the "green" tests established by the recommender and online communities, they may be banished from bidding altogether.

Imagine hundreds of thousands of marketplaces of collaborative consumers with complete information about the products and services they are interested in buying, free from the puffery of advertising and free from the overhyping of salespersons and the underdelivery of performance. Imagine hundreds of thousands of marketplaces of collaborative consumers with oligopsony power: the power to demand that vendors who call on them must have met certain conditions, including a serious effort to reduce carbon emissions and visible proof that they have done so; executive salaries no greater than a predetermined multiple of the wages of the lowest-paid laborer; and no service centers providing after-sale support located in foreign countries or that use customer response management software.

The Transfer of Wealth

As you might imagine, industrial disruption of this magnitude and pain solving at this exciting level will result in a comparable transfer of wealth. Trillions of dollars formerly in the hands of stockholders and managers of corporations on the New York Stock Exchange and similar exchanges will transfer to the founding entrepreneurs and stockholders of online communities and mobile social networks.

Let's take five of the largest consumer products companies in the world: Procter & Gamble, Johnson & Johnson, Kimberly Clark, Merck, and Novartis. Exhibit 6.1 shows how they will be reshaped in the next five years.

The difference between their Gross Profit Margins and their Net Operating Margins is their expenditures on Selling, General and Administrative Expenses (SG&A) plus Research and Development. The SG&A expenses of Procter & Gamble for its trailing 12 months was 31.4 percent of revenues or $25 billion; of that, $3.5 billion was spent on advertising. We have to make assumptions about selling, marketing commissions, and public relations costs, but let's

EXHIBIT 6.1 Transforming the Operating Statements of Five Huge Consumer Products Companies

($billions)	Five-Co Composite	P&G	J&J	Kimberly	Merck	Novartis
Market Caps	126	204	182	27	104	114
Revenue	45	80	61	18	24	40
Gross Profit Margins	60.7%	51.8%	70.9%	31.7%	76.6%	72.5%
Net Optg. Margins	31.3%	20.3%	24.9%	15.0%	25.8%	20.4%

say they were approximately the same as advertising, or $3.5 billion per year. The aggregate of Procter & Gamble's antelope-hunt costs are approximately $7 billion a year. If recommender communities can find customers for Procter & Gamble, then its $7 billion budget will be slashed considerably, and prices can fall by that amount; and Procter & Gamble will lower the prices of its products as a result of community demands to do so. Its revenues—if consumers rate its products highly, a big *if*—will decline by about 5 to 10 percent (depending on the communities' demands) and its Gross Profit Margin will fall proportionately.

What happens to some of the $7 billion? It becomes distributed among the founders, stockholders, and members of recommender online communities and mobile social networks. And that is just the case study for one consumer products company. The antelope-hunt expenditures that will be transferred as newly- earned wealth by the participants in recommender communities for all five companies in Exhibit 6.1 are estimated at $18 billion. Now, put a market/revenue multiple of 30 on $18 billion, and you get $540 billion for a handful of successful recommender online communities. Eventually, this new steamroller called the *recommender social network* will make Google's market capitalization of $140 billion look like a pittance.

Being on the Winning Team

If I am right, if my "call" (a Wall Street term), recommender social networks, is going to become the next giant industry, then clearly you will want to launch and operate or invest in or be a very early employee of a recommender reverse-auction online community or mobile social network. You will want to be the *whom* among those to whom the wealth of Fortune's 5,000 is transferred; those with the power to bring prices down to the marginal profit level and those that have enforcement power to force producers to reduce carbon emissions and gainsay dealing with countries that do not meet the ethical standards set by your community. I will show you how to do that.

In my book, *Smart-Start-ups: How Entrepreneurs and Corporations Can Profit by Starting Online Communities* (Hoboken, NJ: John Wiley & Sons, 2007), I take the ideas of exceptional thinkers such as Benkler, Harford, Schumpeter, and Suroweicki and the numbers generated by the research firms, and get down to where the rubber hits the road—my pocketbook. I am an angel investor in start-up online communities trying to hit more winners than losers. I have given you more than 18 sustainable and relevant revenue channels that include tip jars, reputation management fees, product branding fees, slicing and dicing the conversations of the members, and more, because if the communities that I invest in adopt them and execute them efficiently, then a venture capital round can be avoided because the communities will grow with members' float. Disruption of the venture capital industry will also be achieved by the growth of online communities that adopt the revenue channels that I espouse. So, be sure to send me your recommender online community ideas to dsilver@sfcapital.com. Let's see if you are thinking up winners.

You will be a disrupter, because that is the line of guards, tackles, and ends that will drive the antelope hunters back on their heels or, hopefully, flat on their Polo-clad butts, enabling the painsolver—the quarterback, halfback, and fullbacks—to crash through the line and chew up 10, 20, 30 yards, and cross the goal line.

7

Should You Sell, or Are You Having Too Much Fun?

The Question of Using a Broker

Since the beginning of recorded time, in fact since Isaac transferred his property to his son Jacob and bypassed Esau, the measure of value of one's property has been the subject of considerable debate and discussion. The Bible tells many stories of profitable exit strategies, and not just *Exodus*.

In biblical times, a man's property included his land, animals, slaves, wife, and daughters. Selling these assets occasionally required the advice of rabbis. One section of the *Talmud*, or Jewish book of laws, instructs us that a man can acquire a wife from her father either personally or through an agent. Yet in another section of the *Talmud*, Rabbi Yehuda argues that to acquire a wife through an agent is preferable so that he may hear a report of her dowry and beauty. The rabbi writes, "One is prohibited to be betrothed to a woman before he has seen her, for upon seeing her he may find something repugnant in her and she may be detestable to him." The rabbis of old make a strong case today for using the services of a broker to handle the sale of one's business; yet this point of view remains the subject of debate in modern times.

Some business owners regard a merger and acquisition broker as a hybrid creature, a combination of the biblical Paul and Strato, Brutus's faithful servant in Shakespeare's *Julius Caesar*, who holds Brutus's sword as Brutus runs upon it to kill himself. They see the merger and acquisition broker as an android who shuffles between a file of bottom fishers and a database of buyers and who fills the air with fatuous import and opinion, fully bereft of substance. And some merger and acquisition brokers fit this description well.

The debate concerning the transfer of property, with or without the assistance of a broker, is as old as the concept of property itself. You will see that when a seller accepts cash or assets that can be immediately converted to cash in exchange for his or her business, the value cannot be challenged later on. But when there is a *back-end payment* (which can take one of four forms: a note; a royalty based on sales; an *earn-out*—a percentage of the company's earnings paid to the seller; or a noncompete agreement) disputes are common. Just as the *Talmud* contains conflicting points of view concerning selling a person's assets, there are differences of opinion thousands of years later on the same subject.

The "Theater" of the Sale

Gift-giving is common in primitive societies. Among the Malekula tribe in the New Hebrides, "Entrance to a grade necessitates payments, often on a *large* scale, by the aspirant to those who are already members of it . . . these are made in pigs . . . one pig for . . . a carved wooden image." Valuable objects are owned temporarily in primitive society rather than possessed. Some are too large to wear and too valuable to hang in the tent. "Yet owners get from them a special kind of value pleasure by the mere fact of being entitled to them."

Possession of wealth is considered honorable, and it is the endeavor of each Indian to acquire a fortune. But it is not so much the possession of wealth as the ability to give great festivals that makes wealth desirable to the Indians. The society pages of local newspapers, fashion newspapers, and chic magazines portray the happy faces of the country's financial buyers—private equity fund managers—enjoying festive balls in honor of their gifts to the local art museum, paid for with the cash flows of companies whose owners sold out on the cheap.

The Malekula of primitive society are the financial buyers of today. They acquire companies to create personal wealth, not because the companies they acquire are strategic fits with their businesses but because they *can*. They're smart about cleaning the fat out of the companies they buy. And with their personal wealth they give great festivals for important charities and achieve great renown in their communities. The possession of companies to the financial buyer is a stepping stone to achieving rank in society, crossing the line from nouveau riche to gift-giver to the community.

If you are planning the sale of your company, you will likely meet the modern version of the Malekula who will attempt to lure you into his or her web with the lullaby of *leverage*. But these are just words. Read David Mamet's 1984 Pulitzer Prize—winning play, *Glengarry Glen Ross*, and listen to Ricky Roma hypnotize a naïf with perfectly targeted gibberish:

> A guy comes up to you, you make a call, you send in a brochure, it doesn't matter.
>
> "There're these *properties* I'd like for you to see." What does it mean? What you want it to mean.
>
> Money?
> If that's what it signifies to you.
> Security?
> Comfort?
> All it is is THINGS THAT HAPPEN to you.
> That's all it is. How are they different?

> All it is, it's a carnival. What's special . . . what *draws* us?
> We're not the same.

Rent the DVD of *Glengarry Glen Ross* before selecting a broker to sell your company. It's a classic. It will toughen your fibers.

Stirrups

With the invention of the stirrup in the fourth century, ownership of private property and the attendant issues of selling it became a paramount catalyst in shaping social organization. The stirrup enabled men to wear armor on horseback. Men who could afford armor became formidable; they subdued men who fought on foot. The small farmer, who could not afford armor, became either a serf or a craftsman who made armor for the lord who captured his land. The discovery of the stirrup changed landholding patterns and the control of wealth for centuries to come. More blood has been spilled over property disputes in the subsequent years than as a result of any other single causal factor.

The clash of arms that arose from property disputes is similar in *form* to the clash of values as seen by the seller and the buyer, and the dichotomy between the seller's desire to sell and start another business, with society's newly anointed and revered private equity fund managers and you may be forced to take a large part of your payment in the form of a back-end payment, which is not something I would like to see you accept.

The Financial Buyer's Stirrup

The transfer of ownership of valuable assets has become significantly less sanguinary and more fluid with the development in the early 1970s of the *leveraged buyout* (LBO). The new stirrup is leverage: borrowed money. With it, buyers can borrow on the assets of your company—its recurring revenue streams, its membership base, its brand—which they seek to acquire by paying you upfront cash plus a back-end payment, and then repay their borrowings from the acquired company's cash flow. Management teams of online communities can use the LBO stirrup as well. They can buy the companies they have worked for but never owned, and ambitious young men and women who have served in large corporations can join the Association of Parents of Trust Fund Children by buying profitable companies using the modern stirrup—the LBO.

This creates more opportunities for owners of privately held companies to find eager buyers willing to pay the price they seek, indeed, sometimes in the owner's opinion more than the true worth of the business. But beware of financial buyers. They will in most cases offer you less and tie you up more than *strategic buyers* and cause you more worry about the back-end payment. *The most profitable exit strategy is an all-cash sale to a strategic buyer.*

The Measure of Value

There is no simple rule or formula for valuing a privately held company, but owners can use certain strategies to maximize their selling price. To "learn you all my experiences" in the merger and acquisition business, as Yogi Berra described what Bill Dickey taught him about catching, you must first regard the sale of your business as an *intellectual game*, or if you are more systems-oriented, as a *process*. Games have winners and losers. I believe I can set forth the rules, fundamentals, and tactics for selling your company for the highest price and on the most favorable terms in a clear and concise manner.

Here are six rules to keep in mind about the sale of your company.

1. *Do not listen to free advice.* A community of experts toils daily in the merger and acquisition marketplace—brokers, attorneys, accountants, and appraisers—and provides advice that is worth far more than any tips you pick up from your stockbroker, company or personal attorney, tax accountant, or country club know-it-all, who just sold his or her company for *millions* but hasn't picked up the tab for lunch since his or her hole-in-one in 1996.

2. *Do not discuss your plans with relatives.* The sale of a business is a strategic process like a battle in a war; the watchword is *secrecy*. From beginning to end, everyone involved in helping you sell your business must promise to be bound by an oath of confidentiality. Relatives may not appreciate the need for secrecy. However, since they probably cannot contribute much constructive advice, why tell them anything?

3. *Do not develop an inflated idea of your company's worth.* At the very least, your company is worth its *liquidation value*: the price that its tangible assets would bring at auction. This value can be quickly obtained by hiring a knowledgeable investment banker, and if you own a good brand name and a lot of members, a good business appraiser. These appraisals, net of the company's liabilities, will provide you with the bottom—that is, the lowest all-cash price that you should consider from a buyer. To that, you can add the intrinsic values of the company as a going concern: its cash flow to a new owner; franchise; customer list; intellectual properties such as trademarks, patents, copyrights, tooling, and blueprints; and trained, experienced managers, department heads, and employees. What are they worth? That is one of the answers I intend to provide.

4. *Look for a strategic buyer before you sell to a financial buyer.* A strategic buyer is a company in your industry or a related industry

that seeks to acquire your company for strategic purposes. These purposes might include extending the product line, expanding vertically toward the consumer or toward a source of supply, or finding a new marketing channel for its products. For instance, cable television carriers should be acquiring social network companies to add potential new subscribers. Newspaper publishers should be as well.

On the other hand, a financial buyer will pay a little cash upfront, plus an amount equal to the amount it can leverage on your company's assets plus a back-end payment. The financial buyer will offer you less than the strategic buyer and should be considered only when your company cannot attract a strategic buyer. The problems of selling to a strategic buyer are, of course, finding a merger and acquisition broker who can locate a buyer and maintaining confidentiality when disclosing your financial records and private information.

5. *No one ever lost money selling too soon.* This axiom ties into the tendency of owners of private companies to overvalue the worth of their businesses. Although an early offer may seem too little, it may be the only one you receive. If you reject it out of hand, you may never sell your company, and your heirs may not be able to carry on without your wealth.

6. *Consider selling to the public.* If the strategic buyers are dawdling over your company and the financial buyers are trying to structure the back-end payment with frankincense and myrrh, consider selling to the *public* depending on the frothiness of the initial public offering market. It is currently non-frothy.

The Arbitrage Flips

Strategic buyers will always pay more for your social network than will financial buyers. The latter are seeking a short-term capital gain, or to siphon cash out of your company via dividends.

Sometimes financial buyers will see an arbitrage opportunity that you will not be aware of. *Arbitrage* means that something can be purchased inexpensively in one market and sold dearly in another market. For example, Indian artifacts are plentiful in pawnshops and antique shops in Arizona and New Mexico, and Harley Davidson accessories are plentiful in the Milwaukee area. You could buy the Indian artifacts inexpensively in the Southwest and sell them at a dear price in Milwaukee, and use the cash to buy Harley mud flaps, caps, handlebar streamers, and jackets, and sell them at a profit in the Southwest.

In a market where ideas and strategic thinkers are on every street corner, three people deep, such as New York City or San Francisco, a financial buyer may have heard that a publishing company or a media giant wants to acquire its way into the online community business, but doesn't know where to begin.

The financial buyer prepares a mass mailing to the CEOs of several hundred social networks offering to acquire them. It receives two dozen positive responses, exchanges Confidential Nondisclosure Agreements, does due diligence on the prospective sellers' books and records, and buys five of them for five times EBITDA. Let's say the cash flow (which is the same as EBITDA, that is, "earnings before interest, taxes, depreciation, and amortization") of the five social networks totals $5 million.

The financial buyer pays $25 million for the lot, but borrows 3.5 × EBITDA to pay for them, which is the typical ratio used by lenders in LBOs. Cash flow lenders (those that do not require collateral, but charge 13 percent interest plus warrants on their loans) will generally loan a respectable buyer 3.5 × EBITDA. In this example, the financial buyer borrows $17.5 million and invests $7.5 million of its own money. Once it owns the five social networks it may or may not make some changes. If it finds that some of the acquired companies can continue operating without their founders, it may allow them to leave or terminate them with three-to-five-year noncompete agreements. The buyer may release some nepotistic employees and perhaps save a salary here or there, usually in the accounting department. Let's assume, then, that the buyer saves $1 million by cleaning out the fat.

He then contacts several dozen prospective buyers of online communities and sells all five of his portfolio companies for 10 × EBITDA. The financial buyer grosses $60 million, repays its cash flow lender $17.5 million, and after transaction fees of $1 million, it pockets a profit of $41.5 million. That's known as an *arbitrage flip*. You don't have to be flipped if you can find a strategic buyer.

Why Do Strategic Buyers Always Pay More?

Whereas financial buyers invest in or acquire companies for the purpose of achieving significantly higher-than-conventional returns, in a short period of time, for taking significantly greater-than-typical investment risks, strategic buyers invest in or buy entrepreneurial companies for the following reasons:

To incubate their investments and reduce the cost of acquiring them

To gain exposure to possible new markets

To add new products to existing distribution channels

To reduce the cost of research and development through strategic partnering

To expose middle management to entrepreneurship

To obtain a management training area for bright young trainees in need of experience

To utilize excess capacity, space, or computer time

To mesh the activities of several departments in joint efforts

To generate capital gains

To sit on the windowsill of the acquiring company thus to develop antennae for break through opportunities

To generate income through strategic partnering

To provide excellent group therapy for senior management

To create good public relations by reflecting forward-looking management

To keep pace with their competition, who are probably doing the same thing

To buy back a team that left them to do a start-up

To discuss something new at board meetings

These reasons, given to me by corporate officials who buy entrepreneurial companies, are not all-inclusive, but they are the ones most often cited in descending order by the most active strategic partners.

Positioning Your Company

Finding strategic buyers is difficult. Many of their strategic development officers—the managers who review acquisition candidates—will not want to risk losing their jobs by paying 20 times revenue for your recommender social network. The multiple scares them. The price you are asking them to pay makes them break out into a cold sweat. They want to keep their jobs more than they want to be possible heroes. Thus, it will take some selling on your part. And some considerable preparation. First, you must position your company to be acquired.

Positioning means getting it into the best possible position to receive the best possible price. Let's assume that the price you want is 20 times revenue. You will need some comparable sales to show that $20.0\times$ trailing 12-month revenues is not out of market, but pretty much the norm. There are some blogs that cover trans-actions in the social network industry. The best is prepaidcontent.com. Venture Wire, owned by the *Wall Street Journal*, does an excellent job as well.

Second, in the year before selling your community you will want to run it as lean as possible. Cut out the fat whenever you find it. Assign very high goals to your sales team to accelerate membership growth. Online communities aren't the first indus-try sector to be acquired on a per-membership basis. In the hey-day of magazines and newspapers, they were bought and sold for $600 to $1,000 per subscriber. Neighborhood pharmacies are often priced for sale on a per-customer-prescription basis; the greater the number of prescription customers, the higher the price.

Third, it's not just the number of members that your com-munity has, it's also the delta factor: that is, its rate of change. A 20 percent annual membership growth over the past 5 years will generate a far higher purchase price than will a 10 percent annual membership growth rate.

Fourth, a high renewal rate is critical as well. If members drop off at less than a 5 percent annual rate, you will be in far better shape to command a high price for your community than if the rate is double that number. If your drop out rate is more than 5 percent, then introduce some incentives to revive it.

Fifth, do not discuss the possible sale of your community with anyone except board members. If it leaks out, the gossip will be mostly negative. The presumption that the sale is for negative reasons will be passed from employee to employee, and their work will be less than competent as they worry about their future. Résumés will be written on your time. The esprit de corps that you built so carefully will collapse as fast as the giant slid down the beanstalk.

How Do You Locate Strategic Buyers?

It really isn't so difficult: Who needs to turn around their fortunes immediately? Newspaper publishers come to mind. Media companies such as News Corporation, Walt Disney, Viacom, IAC/InterActiveCorp, General Electric, Time Warner, and the Washington Post Co. all need to break into the serious online community business (not the Facebook, MySpace, Bebo section). Walt Disney acquired Club Penguin. The *New York Times* acquired About.com. There is the beginning of a pattern.

Foreign media and publishing companies such as Lagardere, The Financial Times, and Reed Elsevier can buy American companies with 67-cent dollars. Companies look less expensive to them if they buy in euros or British pounds. A sales trip to Europe could be the best money you ever spent.

Advertising agencies such as WPP, Omnicom, and Interpublic need to be thinking about the vast changes that recommender online communities will cause to their business models. If they buy five or six of them and observe their impact on the old antelope-hunt model, it could ease the disruption that inevitably will occur, by drawing experiences and cash flow from the acquired communities.

In summary, the most likely acquirers are the companies listed in Exhibit 7.1.

EXHIBIT 7.1   Most Likely Acquirers of Your Online Community

American Media Operations
Belo Corporation
Bertelsmann A.
CanWest Global Communications
CBS Corporation
Daily Journal Company
DreamWorks SKG

E.W. Scripps
Editis
Emmis Communications
Gannett Co. Inc.
Gemstar–TV Guide
General Electric Co.
Gray Television
Grupo Televisa
Hearst Newspapers
IDG Corporation
IFC Companies
John Wiley & Sons, Inc.
Journal Communications
Journal Register
Knight Ridder
Lagardere Group SCA
Lee Enterprises
Lions Gate Entertainment Corp.
Martha Stewart Living Omnimedia
McClatchy Company
Media General
MediaNews Group
Meredith
Miramax Film Corp.
News Corporation
New York Times
Pearson, Plc
Playboy Enterprises
PRIMEDIA
Pulitzer Publishing
Quebecor
Random House, Inc.
Reader's Digest Association
Reed Elsevier Group, Plc
Rogers Communications
Thomson Reuters

(Continued)

EXHIBIT 7.1 (*Continued*)

Time Warner, Inc.
Torstar
Transcontinental Group
Tribune Company
Viacom, Inc.
Walt Disney Co.
Washington Post Co.
Ziff Davis Media

8

Wrap-Up

MANY OF TODAY'S BABY BOOMERS joined the workforce in the 1970s with an abhorrence of corporate life. They wanted to do their own thing from the start, and sought the means of solving some of the country's problems in a variety of ways. The opportunities to do things entrepreneurially were enhanced because the federal government had spent itself into moribundity and was beginning to think in terms of doing less, rather than more, to influence change. At the same time the baby boomers realized that being against everything would not put food on the table, and they began to seek positive areas in which to channel their dissatisfaction. They wanted to do several things at once, such was their energy level: Solve society's problems, avoid the corporate handcuffs, and achieve personal wellness. Today's boomers launched the entrepreneurial tsunami that accelerated with the invention of the semiconductor, followed in 1986 by the Internet and in 1995 by the Web.

Why You Are Reading This Book?

Because you are truly an entrepreneur. Entrepreneurs are people dissatisfied with their career paths (though not with their chosen fields) who decide to make their marks on the world by developing and selling products or services that will make life easier for a large number of people.

Social network entrepreneurs are energetic, single-minded, and have missions and clear visions. You intend to create out of your visions a new service, embedded in an online community that will serve a central human need and improve the lives of millions. Although you will probably make a lot of money if the solution works and it is efficiently conveyed to the problems, you do not care. You are delighted to have your heart back, to be free of dissatisfaction and frustration, and to be working action-packed 16-hour days for yourself.

Thus, until the time that you developed the insight into large problems searching for solutions, you worked fully within the scope of traditional societal values, perhaps for a corporation, a government, a medical laboratory, or a consulting firm. You had been hired, you believed, for your creative potential and were rewarded, you believed, for your creative contributions. The satisfaction was not to last long.

Initially you trusted the organizations that valued you and rewarded you principally for your creative output. You had joined these organizations in part because of their prestige; however, as you became more energetic and needed increasing latitude and funding for your inventions, the organizations' commitments to your personal creative potentials emerged as less than you wanted, less than you expected. At first surprised, you became increasingly dissatisfied.

At the same time, as trust in the workplace faded, a strong commitment to your own capabilities was unfolding. More and more, you experienced a sense of directedness; your inner voices were asking you questions about personal values, expression of self-worth, and self-sufficiency. These were not the abstract philosophical stock-taking questions that observers and analysts of midlife change report have been raised so frequently: questions like, "What have I accomplished in my life?" "What have I sacrificed?" "What will I do with the rest of my life?" Those questions are as likely to come to entrepreneurs as to anyone else. But at this point in your life, the big question was: "What will I do with my creativity?"

You were intense, deadly serious about homesteading somewhere and being able to exercise confidence in yourself. Before you even knew it had started, the entrepreneurial race was on. For a time, as you continued to do your job for your employers, dissatisfaction increased while ideas for the products or services you would develop—that would take the marketplace by storm— were putting down roots in your mind. Although the first growths might be primary shoots that wither, the root systems were secure, come sunny weather or violent storm. And you will be protected by enormous potential to replenish psychic energy, by intense pleasure at your activity, and if you are to be successful, by excellent communication skills and exquisite judgment.

Complex, Determined, Imaginative People

You ask yourself, however, "Have I picked the right stage to carry out my play?" With so many serious problems cascading against one another from mortgage fraud to the clogged credit markets and from stock market meltdowns to global warming, will a start-up be a distraction to potential members and possible strategic partners and not worthy of their time and attention? There are two answers to this question, and they tie back to Schumpeter: *disrupt* and *solve pain.*

If your community disrupts an existing marketplace it will get attention—possibly from heavy-footed lawyers of the corporations that have been disrupted. But that is a good thing. Send the letters to all the relevant online and offline business journalists, and embarrass those who threatened you.

And then, your community must solve pain. If it merely links teenager A to teenager B, you're wasting your time and talent. You must be a pain solver to be an authentic, credible entrepreneur.

I meet many entrepreneurs at this stage of their growth when they want to discuss their ideas with an older hand. All of them are complex, intense, determined, imaginative people who have faith in themselves, and whose energy is not sapped by pervasive anger, bitterness, or disappointment. Their workplaces have not been satisfying, or true, and have not rewarded what they most respect in themselves; the not-yet-active entrepreneurs have put in a lot of time and tried to contribute their best. They have become dissatisfied and to some extent disillusioned. And they are not politically adept, so their pure commitment to human potential irritates rather than inspires management, making it impossible for them to maneuver budgets and forums of influence the way others can to make the organizational dynamics work for, not against, them.

Nevertheless, though they resent the system, they proceed despite their disillusion and go on to create their own reality; thus, true entrepreneurs do not feel victimized. They do not plot and plan retaliation. Rather, they accept that these organizations will not provide places to do what they want to do and believe should be done, and they decide to create such an organization of their own.

Acceptance of reality brings determination, not depression, distraction, or diffuse, flailing attempts to get even, to show up their opponents. (They have others to "show," as we will see later on.) Acceptance brings dedication to building on their own strengths rather than to demonstrating the weakness of the organization (and thereby deluding themselves that it would change anything with respect to their positions). They know that it is difficult to reduce corporate power, so they decide to establish their own disrupter and pain solver.

The personal goals and needs that have been emerging as the strongest forces soon take over to govern their behavior. They direct their psychic and creative energy into building on the emotional self-sufficiency that has been slowly, steadily taking hold. They do this with an ease that astounds people who know or hear about them.

The creative intelligence they brought to their employers' businesses is now directed toward designing social networks and positioning them for the marketplace. They examine opportunities, perhaps for introducing an online community in the field in which they have been working, see nothing available, and may work for a short time as independent consultants or for consulting firms. During this time the entrepreneurs continue to see the needs they identified and finally decide to create their own opportunities.

They are getting ready to break ground, carve out niches, and build places in the sun. "Build places in the sun," I said, not "build empires"; empire building is not what they are about. Rather, they are planning for, and are after, self-reliance, a quality-controlled platform for creative output. A niche is found. It starts to feel that harmony is adhering to melody. They talk about building an organization where people will not get lost; where creativity will be rewarded; where salaries and benefits will be just; where participative management (though they do not call it by that name) will be the rule, not the exception. To the amazement of people who were not able to turn anger, energy, disappointment, and dissatisfaction into focused personal directedness, they begin to experience intense pleasure. The undercurrent of basic optimism and trust in their professional power, the certainty that has always existed that their expertise in their fields is unequaled, governs a clear decision to be on their own and succeed. They have no fear of failure, though they make careful, detailed plans to avoid it. Statistics of new business and small business failure offered to them by well-meaning friends and family are dismissed as irrelevant.

"Sure, lots of people fail, but since I'm going to succeed, why are you telling me these numbers?" they ask, before going on with their phone calls to bankers, brokers, angels, and friends, and with presentations end to end. Failure is simply not a possibility. They have spotted opportunities and are leaping forward to take advantage of them.

With confidence, optimism, courage, focus, and determination, newly born entrepreneurs set out to look for money. What happens then depends on whether they possess two other attributes; it seems to correlate as well with several factors in their childhood home lives. Did they develop judgment from a parent or mentor? Are they patient, an attribute of people raised with siblings?

To build successful businesses, would-be entrepreneurs must be able to lead their teams by exercising good judgment—knowing the *right thing* to do at the right time. But since they may not have a clue about how to do the things right, they will eventually get tangled up in the snare of trying to plan businesses. Without knowing word one about functional areas like strategic planning, sales projections, market research, or even simple accounting practices, they will at this point select managers who do and who can allow the entrepreneur chieftains to maintain leadership.

I have seen the most talented entrepreneurs select high school or college friends to be their chief operating officers without asking them if they had the goods. The result was failure.

The higher entrepreneurs reach for managers, the more likely are their businesses to succeed. Entrepreneurs exhibit the keen judgment they are known for when they ask achievers to join them—people who have demonstrated first-class management ability in a growth situation.

To raise the angel capital that will launch the new businesses, entrepreneurs must be able to make and keep the process simple, and to convince others it is so.

What might make others topple into confusion and frantic despair nourishes their spirit and spirited intellect. Out of the complexity they pull the necessary interim funding from the most unlikely sources—usually on the day the bank loan interest is due; first-rate presentations to angel groups; corps of dedicated partners or colleagues; determination and confidence enough to refuse equity-hungry venture tempters. Those would-be entrepreneurs who have judgment and patience and business acumen will become wealthy; those who do not will be wiped out in the marketplace.

Community-Building Heroes

You know who some of the well-known personalities are, those who have told of transformations overnight, abrupt decisions to do something that their hearts commanded them to do.

Bob Crull, who segued from web hosting and without capital, but pure grit and "vapor from a turpentine rag," as they say in Oklahoma, built OneSite.com into the leading builder and maintainer of online communities. Dr. Daniel Palestrant spotted doctors' increasing sense of isolation, and founded Sermo.com to provide them with a safe community to openly discuss medical solutions by bouncing queries off of the wisdom of crowds. Kathy Kelley of Denton, Texas founded hystersisters.com in 1998 as a forum where women would come to discuss gynecological problems and has guided it steadily to one of the greatest pain solvers in the land. Robert Kalin, Chris Maguire, Haim Shoppik, and Jarad Tarbell founded Etsy, where artisans and craftspeople go to sell their handmade objects. It charges a 20-cent listing fee and 3.5 percent sales commission. Etsy has passed two million items sold through its marketplace. And there is Luis van Ahn, of which more will be written soon.

Bob Crull, Kathy Kelley, Daniel Palestrant, and the Etsy founders will someday be as well known as Andrew Grove and Edwin Land: men and women who experience dissatisfaction with their corporate or hierarchical employers, and have not only the insight into problems and their solutions, but also the energy to begin the *chase*—to build companies that will convey their solutions to the problems.

Many people are dissatisfied with their corporate or hierarchical employers and may have important insights. However, lacking the energy to begin the chase, these people indulge in creative hobbies or start side businesses to develop an outlet for their frustration and do something that they can put their hearts into. Writers have many insights into central social problems and frequently feel anguish toward structures that crush creativity. They get their hearts back through their pens and laptops. Entrepreneurs experience the pain, see large problems and unique solutions, and have the energy to build companies to deliver solutions to problems. In so doing, their hearts focus their knowledge and drive them toward their common goal: to solve serious problems for a large number of people.

The Planet's New Heroes

The planet has a new hero, its first since Winston Churchill or Franklin Delano Roosevelt. No, I'm not talking about the traditional entrepreneur. Investment and commercial bankers have embarrassed themselves with the subprime mortgage crisis. And, prior to the election of Barack Obama, the political world wasn't serving up any beauties. The planet's new hero is the social network entrepreneur. Let's define terms.

The word *hero* defines someone who is great—someone who has achieved an authentic instance of greatness. A hero is someone who has intentionally taken a large step, one far beyond the capacities of most persons, in solving a problem that affects an immense number of people. A hero brings about something that is unlikely to have happened by the mere force of events, by the trends or tendencies of the time—that is, something that is unlikely to occur without his or her direct intervention. The planet's new heroes are distinguishable, in the first instance, by the fact that their intervention makes the highly improbable happen.

These great persons do not seek publicity, and as a result are not widely known. They are essentially shy and imprisoned within driven, fanatical personalities. In this involuntary confinement, the heroes have developed a certain independence of outlook. Questions of status, social position, and relative degrees of economic standing—so common in many people—have not affected them. Heroes were often raised by frontier mothers, who were strong and self-possessed with energetic and hopeful attitudes toward life. These mothers had a respect for education, for a fully formed personality, for solid achievement in every sphere, together with a clear-eyed concrete—possibly irreverent—approach to all issues. Above all, they respected effort, honesty, faith, and a critical facility. "Don't be a sinner," they said. "But worse than a sinner, don't be a sucker."

Raised without fathers, in many cases, who were frequently or permanently absent, the children developed contingency plans for self-preservation. Later this would be regarded as courage, resisting failure or downside planning. "Shoot at me," our heroes say to their enemies. "I'm going to succeed anyhow."

Our new heroes know they are stronger, more imaginative, and more effective fighters than their fellow citizens. They are fearless, understanding, and indifferent to praise or blame.

Our heroes build groups of followers by convincing them that their view of the future will become reality. Joining the heroes will improve their lives and shelter them from failure, while enabling them to save a large portion of the planet. The hero and her team have immense natural authority, dignity, and strength.

Their Timing Couldn't Be Better

The peculiar quality of greatness and a sense of the sublimity of the occasion stems from a delight in being alive at the right time and in control of events at a critical moment in history. The planet's new heroes thrive on change and the instability of things. The infinite possibilities of the unpredictable future offer endless opportunities for spontaneous moment-to-moment improvisation and for their large, imaginative, bold strokes that cause important events that change the course of history. Although strength comes to our heroes from their clear, brightly colored vision of— and passionate faith in—their views of the future and in their power to mold it, they know where they are going, by what means, and why. This strength enhances their energy and drive as it did Winston Churchill's during the Battle of Britain when he said: "It is impossible to quell the inward excitement which comes from a prolonged balancing of terrible things" (Isaiah Berlin, *Personal Impressions* [New York: Viking, 1981]).

The immense problems for which our heroes will soon be designing, developing, and implementing solutions using the online community and mobile social network business models are global warming and terrorism.

Normally, entrepreneurs, of which social network entrepreneurs are a subset, either create new companies that disrupt existing industries or create companies that deliver a solution to a problem that solves pain. Social network entrepreneurs get a lot of ink for disrupting existing industries, but that is because the industries they have been disrupting are media and communications, the owners of the ink bottle and the printing press. We read and hear about MySpace, YouTube, and Facebook *ad absurdum*, but they are popular because younger people are seeking to define themselves by their tastes in music, clothing, dates, humor, and the like. Youth often leads, and the algorithms that built these amazing communities are interesting in their value as precursors to how social networks in their most fabulous incarnation will be used to solve the planet's great crises of the moment: *global warming* and *terrorism*. The work is being done in start-up facilities by our heroes and their teams of software engineers and strategic thinkers, far from the view of the media. Drawing attention to themselves would draw outsiders banging on their doors to disrupt their 24/7/365 pace—yes, some of the software engineers are in India and China, clicking away while the Westerners take catnaps.

How Global Warming Will Be Foiled by Social Networks

First of all, it should be said that I am an angel capitalist and privy to thousand of business plans and, therefore, can discuss some of the business plans of the planet's new heroes only in the abstract. Global warming will be foiled by social network entrepreneurs who are adapting very old business models to a very new problem: They are the Minutemen, or more contemporaneously, the neighborhood watch. Dozens of online and mobile communities are being formed using the subscriber-build model. The models will morph into monthly subscription fee and tip-jar models once there are millions of members. The subscription fees will be very affordable—around $5 a month—and the tip jars will collect money for the members who do the best job of reporting to all of the members the names of the carbon emission violators and carbon emission reducers and their recent actions to either save or help destroy the planet. A typical tip might be $20 for, let's say, catching a Midwestern politician running for office touting corn as the cheapest feedstock for making biofuels, when it is far from it.

The tip would be split 70 percent to the reporter and 30 percent to the community owner/operator. If tens of millions of people, seriously concerned about global warming, report violators and salute carbon emission reducers, and do it with guidance from the social network entrepreneurs, the race to save the planet might be won.

The tools to do this are clearly there. If millions of people boycott certain retail gas stations whose parent companies are not converting to biofuels, and if millions of people boycott products made by companies that operate coal-burning factories, and if millions of people boycott the use of plastic water bottles, plastic toys, and plastic baggies made from imported petroleum, then the conversion to biofuels will be accelerated. Some business models that I have seen are promising to invest a significant portion of their profits in biodiesel plants using inexpensive raw materials such as yellow grease— from hamburgers and fast food—trap grease, palm oil, and jatropha oil. If they are effective Minutemen, these communities may sign up 10 million members, and with revenues of $5 a month from their members, that's $600 million a year, and not very much in the way of operating expenses to deduct from that number. If profitability is in the $450 million range, and if a third of that is invested in biodiesel start-ups, a community that organizes its members to fight global warming can become a serious player over a 10-year period with $1.5 billion in anti-global warming investments. It is inevitable that biofuels will overtake petroleum; what is necessary is to hasten the time period before death from the sun do us part.

GreenableWorld.com

GreenableWorld.com, my hypothetical global-warming-battling community, is the first comprehensive consumer-driven web site that is focused on bringing "green" to millions of mainstream users through stimulating consumer activism.

GreenableWorld.com will become an online community that is committed to sustaining the planet. It will be formed by a group of proven business-people to create the definitive clearinghouse of reliable information on the efforts—and more importantly—the lack thereof of corporations, governments, and enterprises on reducing greenhouse gas emissions. It will serve the rapidly growing $40 billion Lifestyles of Health and Sustainability (LOHAS) market by providing consumers with one of the largest collections of green and ecofriendly education, information, products, and services found in one central location.

The business model of GreenableWorld.com will be built around an online community in which the content is user-generated, and paid for on a subscription basis, as well as the use of a tip jar to reward excellence in citizen journalism, an adjunctive synthetic currency called "Greenies" to be used to purchase avatars and outfit them on the GreenableWorld.com web portal, reputation management fees to purchase the company's newsletter, and a management fee to pay for managing the GreenableWorld.com not-for-profit foundation. As membership grows, GreenableWorld.com will add branding, infomercials, prepaid credit cards, and users group meetings to its revenue channels.

The essence of a web portal—based online community, such as J.D. Powers, is that the members will self-regulate and thus assure that the information that is *searched, processed, and shared* within the GreenableWorld.com community will be truthful. This bond of trust has made other communities, such as Wikipedia and eBay, the great successes that they have become. Wikipedia and eBay, as well as Habbo Hotel, Mixi, Second Life, CyWorld, and OhmyNews—all of them online communities based on search-process-share—are successful, have loyal members, employ reputation management tools to keep out defectors, corporate decoys, and griefers, and employ one or more of the following business tools for revenue-generating and reputation management:

Membership subscriptions	Because "membership has its privileges," to borrow a time-honored phrase.
Tip jar	To reward members for excellence in citizen journalism.
Branding	Consumer product companies will introduce new brands through GreenableWorld.com.
Greenies	To create a synthetic currency that is necessary to support the effort to reduce greenhouse gas emissions, and to reward vendors who support the effort of GreenableWorld.com members.
Newsletter subscriptions	The online, continuously updated GreenableWorld.com newsletter will report defectors, and publish the stories of members and news concerning who is sustaining the planet and who is not.
J.D. Powers	GreenableWorld.com will put its "seal of approval" (and charge for it) on products its members vote as authentically green.
Infomercials	GreenableWorld.com will offer to sell its videos of community members gathering to judge products to local evening TV news programs.
Management fee	GreenableWorld.com will form a 501-C3 corporation. As grant money accumulates, the Foundation will make investments in bio fuel start-ups.

Once established, the revenue stream (which the company expects to grow substantially over the next one to five years) will be sustainable for a long period, due to the anticipated ongoing growth of the population that will have an interest in LOHAS and environment-related information, products, and services.

The company plans to make judicious use of consultants and to keep a relatively low employee headcount, further enhancing long-term profitability. Because of its national brand-building activities, thus creating significant demand for its site, as well as aggressive membership recruitment, the company believes it will position itself as one of the core online portals and go-to destinations in the LOHAS market with a recognizable brand.

Pent-Up Demand

GreenableWorld.com will attempt to become *the* definitive company in the emerging marketplace of service organizations that will seek to nucleate concerned citizens anxious to do something positive to sustain the planet—and in turn improve the health and wellness of themselves and their families.

The premise behind GreenableWorld.com is that a very large number of people would very much like to join and participate in a community that is created by a centralized and highly reputable organization that would provide a highly visible platform for ideas and solutions as well as protests and concerns. That centralized and highly reputable organization does not presently exist.

Market researchers have used various terms to describe the current movement; the one most recently coined is "Conscientious Consumerism" by market research firm Packaged Facts. This represents the trend toward upscale and premium products with an ethical bent, and it has taken root across America as consumers increasingly preach their social concerns through their pocketbooks.

Packaged Facts estimates that U.S. retail sales of grocery products making some form of ethical claim reached nearly $33 billion in 2006, an increase of more than 17 percent from 2005. The report projects that sales of products containing ethical elements will maintain double-digit growth over the next five years, surpassing $57 billion in 2011.

It is not surprising that food and beverages dominate retail sales of ethical products with an 82 percent market share. With organics becoming popular in all retail channels, the awareness of ethical edibles has skyrocketed, making hormone-free, pesticide-free, fair-trade, and other ethically labeled foods and beverages widely popular with consumers from all lifestyles.

Major corporations have taken note of ethical products' broad appeal. Manufacturers are creating entirely new ethical product lines and corporations are going green in an effort to build consumer confidence and get a piece of the ethical pie.

"The days of the granola head at a natural food store are gone. Mass-market channels are quickly catching up to the stage set by natural wonders such as Whole Foods and Trader Joe's, a trend which should increase substantially with the entrance of Wal-Mart into the ethical marketplace," notes Don Montuori, the publisher of Packaged Facts.

According to the *New York Times* and the *LOHAS (Lifestyles of Health and Sustainability) Journal*, sales of natural products, including food and personal care products, were $36 billion (2005) in the United States, up from $14.8 billion five years earlier. This market includes more than 25 percent of American adults and is 50 million strong.

GreenableWorld.com will create tools for its users and members to create and post relevant articles and materials, including personal blogs, photo galleries, videos, Greenies, lockers, and wristbands to build loyalty. The information-sharing opportunity at GreenableWorld.com will be a means for committed members to contact and engage each other. This feature has proven to be highly successful on other sites such as MySpace.com and Digg.com.

Another goal is to create strong interest in the community from ecofriendly merchants, who have e-commerce capabilities to test their brands and to pay for brand launches.

GreenableWorld.com should set its goal to become the most trustworthy organization in the save-the-planet market. The task is daunting, but other companies have built trust and authenticity. "Mimic the baker and Starbucks", I wrote earlier.

The *New York Times* has done so in journalism. The *Wall Street Journal* has done so in business journalism. FedEx has captured the truthfulness high ground in promising and then delivering on the promise that one's package will be delivered the next day by 10:30 A.M. McDonald's promised a safe, clean place for working parents to take their families for dinner. CNN calls itself "the most trusted name in news," and when there is a major, life-threatening crisis, it captures about two-thirds of all viewers, to the dismay of the three networks, plus CNBC and Fox News. Wal-Mart promises always low prices, and it delivered on the promise so convincingly that it massively disrupted the retailing industry.

There are other examples of companies that successfully nucleated pent-up demand for a scarce resource, and when that resource was made available, consumers flocked to it. GreenableWorld.com will seek to emulate these successful businesses, and to provide one central, reliable place for people who are concerned about the planet to go and *search, process, and share*.

The Need That the Company Is Addressing

GreenableWorld.com is addressing an enormous and growing need. If it succeeds in establishing itself as the de facto leading online resource for the millions of people looking to curb global warming and improve health and wellness for themselves and their families, the company could become one of the most successful businesses and brands of the new generation.

If you accept the assumption that many people want to do something about saving the planet, and if you also assume that the free enterprise system welcomes customers and provides capital and rewards high valuations for corporations such as ADP, 3M, Amazon.com, Genentech, American Express, and Google (all of which have solved big problems and disrupted industries in the process), then it is reasonable to assume that if GreenableWorld. com *executes* its business model efficiently, it will become a successful corporation.

Site Features

GreenableWorld.com will offer members and users the following benefits:

- Local Green Guides to help users find information/businesses in the following areas:
  - Events (hikes, clean-up days, and so on)
  - Green/environmental nonprofit organizations
  - Environmental government agencies (city, state, and so on)
  - Restaurants powered by solar panels
  - Farmers' markets
  - Naturopathic/homeopathic clinics
  - Green veterinarians (offering non-traditional treatment)
  - Classes on energy-saving techniques
  - Fair trade/organic coffee cafes
  - Green building suppliers
  - Recycling centers
  - County/city recycling programs

- Green gardening supplies, with rate, review, and recommend placards affixed to the products voted on as most green by the community
- Green professional services (architects, and so on)
- Boutiques featuring eco friendly/green products
- Green household services (nontoxic carpet cleaners, furnace/vent cleaning, landscapers, and so on)
- All-natural pet stores/services (dog wash, and so on)
- Jobs in sustainability/green organizations
- Volunteer section (get involved/engaged)
- Parents can rate, review, and recommend with other parents as well as experts regarding natural, organic, and ecofriendly food, clothing, and products for babies and children. Winners and losers will be announced in the newsletters.
- Companies and organizations can use the free member profile to actively promote and educate other users about their products and/or services.
- The community will actively promote the benefits of incorporating aspects of green lifestyle in daily life and demonstrates how real people use green solutions/products in their lives.
- The site will be a resource for users of all ages, ranging from students and teachers who will be able to turn to it as a resource for the growing number of science/environmental projects required, to parents and other adults who will use it as an extension of their daily lives.
- Ongoing fresh content (in the form of posted articles, product reviews, blog posts, and related material) will ensure that the site never gets stale or users bored with the site.

Cash Flow Statement Projections

The Company's first three years' cash flow statement projections are shown in Exhibit 8.1.

EXHIBIT 8.1 GreenableWorld.com Cash Flow Statement Projections: Year One

($000s)	Mo. 1	Mo. 2	Mo. 3	Mo. 4	Mo. 5	Mo. 6	Mo. 7	Mo. 8	Mo. 9	Mo. 10	Mo. 11	Mo. 12	Total Yr. 1
Members Cum.	1,000	2,000	5,000	8,000	12,000	17,000	22,000	27,000	32,000	37,000	42,000	47,000	47,000
Revenues:													
Newsletter	-	-	-	-	-	-	-	54	64	74	84	92	368
Sponsors	-	-	-	-	6	8	22	27	48	56	84	94	345
Tip Jar	-	-	-	-	5	-	5	5	8	8	8	10	49
Affiliate Net	-	-	-	-	-	-	-	-	-	-	-	14	14
Recommend	-	-	-	-	-	-	-	-	20	-	-	40	60
Total Revenues	-	-	-	-	11	8	27	86	140	138	176	250	836
Optg. Expenses:													
Commty Build.	50	-	50	15	15	15	15	15	15	15	15	15	235
Servers	-	-	20	-	-	-	-	-	-	-	-	-	20
Systems Engs.	20	24	26	28	30	32	34	34	34	34	34	45	375
SEO, e-mktg.	-	-	-	10	15	20	25	30	35	40	60	65	300
Telecom	5	5	5	5	5	5	10	10	10	10	10	10	90
Misc. Prof.	-	-	5	5	5	5	5	5	5	5	5	5	50
Total Optg. Expenses	75	29	106	63	70	77	89	94	89	104	124	140	1070
Net Optg. Income	(75)	(29)	(106)	(63)	(59)	(69)	(62)	(8)	(51)	24	52	110	(234)

EXHIBIT 8.1 (*Continued*) GreenableWorld.com Cash Flow Statement Projections: Year Two

($000s)	Mo. 13	Mo. 14	Mo. 15	Mo. 16	Mo. 17	Mo. 18	Mo. 19	Mo. 20	Mo. 21	Mo. 22	Mo. 23	Mo. 24	Total Yr. 2
Members Cum.	52,000	57,000	62,000	67,000	72,000	77,000	82,000	87,000	92,000	97,000	102,000	107,000	107,000
Revenues:													
Newsletter	104	114	124	134	144	154	164	174	184	194	204	214	1,908
Sponsors	10	11	16	17	18	23	29	30	32	39	41	43	309
Tip Jar	10	10	10	12	12	12	14	14	14	16	16	16	156
Affiliate Net	–	–	19	–	–	23	–	–	27	–	–	31	99
Recommend	–	–	60	–	–	80	–	–	100	–	–	120	360
Total Revenues	124	135	329	163	174	292	207	218	357	249	261	424	2,832
Optg. Expenses:													
Commty Build.	15	15	15	15	15	15	15	15	15	15	15	15	180
Servers	20	–	–	–	–	–	–	–	–	–	–	–	20
Systems Engs.	48	51	54	57	60	63	66	69	72	75	78	81	774
SEO, e-mktg.	65	65	65	65	65	65	65	65	65	65	65	65	780
Telecom	15	15	15	15	15	15	18	18	18	18	18	18	198
Misc. Prof.	6	6	6	6	6	6	7	7	7	7	7	7	76
Total Optg. Expenses	165	152	155	173	161	164	171	174	177	180	186	186	2,028
Net Optg. Income	(41)	(17)	74	(10)	13	128	26	44	180	69	75	238	804

EXHIBIT 8.1 (*Continued*) GreenableWorld.com Cash Flow Statement Projections: Year Three

($000s)	Mo. 25	Mo. 26	Mo. 27	Mo. 28	Mo. 29	Mo. 30	Mo. 31	Mo. 32	Mo. 33	Mo. 34	Mo. 35	Mo. 36	Total Yr. 3
Members Cum.	112,000	117,000	122,000	127,000	132,000	137,000	142,000	147,000	152,000	157,000	162,000	167,000	167,000
Revenues:													
Newsletter	224	234	244	254	264	274	284	294	304	314	324	334	3,014
Sponsors	44	46	48	50	52	54	56	58	60	62	64	66	660
Tip Jar	18	18	18	20	20	20	22	22	22	24	24	24	252
Affiliate Net	–	–	33	–	–	36	–	–	39	–	–	42	150
Recommend	–	–	140	–	–	160	–	–	180	–	–	200	680
Total. Revenues	286	298	438	324	336	544	362	374	605	400	412	66	4,756
Optg. Expenses:													
Commty Build.	15	15	15	15	15	15	15	15	15	15	15	15	180
Servers	20	–	–	–	–	–	–	–	–	–	–	–	20
Systems Engs.	81	81	81	81	81	81	85	85	85	85	85	85	996
SEO, e-mktg.	65	65	65	65	65	65	70	70	70	70	70	70	810
Telecom	20	20	20	20	20	20	20	20	20	20	20	20	240
Misc. Prof.	8	8	8	8	8	8	8	8	8	8	8	8	96
Total Optg. Expenses	209	189	189	189	189	189	194	194	194	194	194	194	2,342
Net Optg. Income	77	109	294	135	147	355	168	180	411	206	218	472	2,414

Fighting Terrorism via a Social Network

Luis van Ahn, the developer of Captchas, which thwart spam-bots, and the winner of a $500,000 MacArthur genius grant, is the first of the planet's new superheroes. A former games developer, van Ahn came up with the idea of blocking spam using games algorithms. He wrote a program that generates five random letters and numbers, distorts them, and places them on a funny background. If a person types in the four funny characters correctly, he gets in. Machines can't do that. Van Ahn called his machine the Completely Automated Public Turing Test to Tell Computers and Humans Apart, or "Captcha." This led him into cryptography, and he started thinking about harnessing everyone with a computer and Internet access to verify each other's output. If two people agreed, then the third was verified. Naturally, he took this assumption and using games algorithms came up with a model by which everyone could be turned into a cyberposse searching for terrorists on the Web. Van Ahn has visited with officials at the Homeland Security Department and pitched his solution. If their response is the typical bureaucratic "do nothing," then surely van Ahn will create an anti terrorism online community on his own. It might look like the one I am about to describe.

The advent of the camera phone and the ease of capturing an event and uploading it to a community of experts with pixel-merging and video authenticating software is in place, and social network entrepreneurs will soon be creating business models as fast as they can to save the planet from jihadists and terrorists. The subscriber-build is the business model of choice, because it is a faster launch, needing word-of-mouth from respected bloggers to fuel the fire. Compensation to members to spot and report a terroristic or murderous event in the making could come from a number of sources, including tip jars, bonuses paid by the communities, and fees charged to the event interruption software providers and the newspaper and newscasters, such as the *New York Times*, CNN, and *Le Monde*, among many others. The key is the authentication process. If the community accepts a video of Pope Benedict being shot, for instance, and it is a paste-up job with his face on someone else's body, poof! There goes the community's reputation. But there are methods for authenticating photos and videos. Plus, the communities can use DRM software to block submittals from griefers or decoys who want to distract or tease serious members from their tasks. The anti-terrorist social network entrepreneurs will necessarily need to build strong reputation management squads and software methods to keep out the anti-anti terrorists from submitting photos and videos: eBay has an outstanding reputation management system and Wikipedia's is getting better every day.

Calamitytower.com

Calamitytower.com, my hypothetical anti-terrorist social network, will become the first and only online community focused on disaster preparedness at the local level and communities that engage a variety of stakeholders including active community members, volunteers, government, media businesses, landlords, developers, local banks, schools, filmmakers, and nonprofits. Calamitytower. com is a social network for people to interact, discuss topics, learn about their area, plan events, and organize community projects. The Calamitytower.com business model leverages community interaction and content creation and includes a variety of revenue streams:

- *Web Sites:* Powered by . . . sponsorships on the home page
- *Affiliate Ad Network:* Local demographically and geotargeted ad network connecting traffic to local newspaper, radio, broadcast, blogs, nonprofits, and government web sites (display and video),

with supplemental integration/maintenance fees as revenue to the company

- *Nonprofit Affiliates:* Called *NFPs*—Integration fees/maintenance fees for applications hosting, marketing services fees, and advertising (display and video), and fund raising
- *National and Local Sponsorship:* The active impact of Calamitytower.com projects providing a highly desirable sponsor positioning at many levels, including product integration into content, co-branding, and affinity marketing
- *Local Business "Affinity Membership":* making local businesses that contribute to local Calamitytower.com projects affinity members and building community loyalty by promoting affiliation with Calamitytower.com
- *Nonprofit Marketing:* Marketing fees for promoting projects and donor opportunities
- *Local Government:* Federal and local grants and program funding
- *Television:* Carriage fees, sponsorship, foreign format and distribution rights

Marketing Strategy

The company will be pursuing three audience-building strategies: (1) viral apps on leading social networks Facebook and "open social"; (2) a "white label" Calamitytower.com-hosted application embedded across partner sites in the verticals of media, blogs, government, nonprofits, and local blogs; and (3) the development of episodic web and television programming featuring Calamitytower.com project competitions.

Commons-Based Peer Production

Social networking is creating the condition that enables Commons-Based Peer Production (CBPP), a term coined by Yochai Benkler to describe the emerging model for production that is enabled by social networking:

> The declining price of communications lowers the cost of peer production and makes human capital the primary economic good involved. [Increasing] the importance of peer productions' relative advantage—identifying the best available human capital in highly refined increments and allocating it to projects.
>
> —Yochai Benkler, "Coase's Penguin,"
> *Yale Law Journal* (2002)

CBPP has recently emerged as a new model of economic production in which the creative energy of large numbers of people is coordinated with the aid of the Internet into large, meaningful projects, mostly without traditional hierarchical organization or financial compensation. Examples of product created by means of commons-based peer production include the Linux open source computer operating system; Slashdot, a news and announcement web site; Kuroshin, a discussion site for technology and culture; Wikipedia, an online encyclopedia; and Clickworkers, a citizen science program.

CBPP is distinct from the traditional production models of "firm" production (where a centralized decision process decides what has to be done and by whom) and "market-based" production (when tagging different prices to different jobs serves as an attractor to anyone interested in doing the job).

Group-Forming Scale

Facebook and eBay have achieved monumental scale in large part due to how their structure allows users to form groups.

Communities that facilitate group-forming networks (GFNs) can scale in accordance with Reed's Law, which states that the utility of large networks that support the creation of communicating social groups scales exponentially. In turn, each Project pivots on a "virtuous cycle" in which each stakeholder derives benefits, which fuels additional projects. This "virtuous cycle" is further augmented by the lowering of organizational and transactional costs derived from the emergence of pervasive mobile communications and the outsized benefit derived from commons-based peer production (such as Linux and Wikipedia). Additional incentives can be added to fuel the local "virtuous cycle":

- The creation of a local merchant affinity rewards club.
- The site gives a percent of sponsorship dollars to the NFP, incentivizing sponsors to "Powered by . . ." slots and incentivizing members to patronize sponsors. This is an indirect way to contribute to the NFP and the Projects. Sponsors get an associational benefit because the Projects deliver a social good. Window stickers are sent to sponsors.
- A point system for members that rewards them based on their level of participation/contribution and recruitment. Rewards could include giving their votes greater weight, eligibility for paying NFP staff positions (such as project coordinator), and invites to special Calamitytower.com events. The point system will also be used to rank the top actively involved subset communities. Subset communities that have the highest number of points from members, organizations, and businesses in the area will become "Calamitytower.com Preferred" communities.
- Incentives in the form of preferred sponsor and ad positioning could be given to sponsors and affiliates that give greater in-kind and monetary contributions.

Business Strategy

Calamitytower.com's strategy is to become the dominant local disaster preparedness network: a dynamic platform where locals build consensus around issues, collaborate to carry out citizen watchdog efforts in local business, universities, schools, and government agencies to be ready to deal with terrorist attacks, psychopathic killers, and chemical spills, among other disasters. This strategy includes creating a demographic, behavioral, and geographic targeted affiliate and sponsorship network comprised of aggregating partner affiliates sites. The company will also build value by developing unscripted episodic web and TV series and an international program format. The content model is open source, meaning that the users may upload programming about projects or even amateur documentaries about local issues.

The company will be structured with a nonprofit affiliate so that direct donations can be received by the nonprofit affiliates to coordinate and supervise projects. Media fees may be allocated to the for-profit media company for promoting projects.

To build audience, Calamitytower.com will follow a three-pronged strategy, including (1) an "open social" and Facebook application that allow a users to express their views on local hot-button issues and virally share with friends; (2) affiliating with existing communities of stakeholders such as cities, local media and blogs, clubs, associations, and nonprofits that focus on local disaster awareness projects; and (3) producing and distributing web and television content to wide audiences.

Strategic Plan

The ultimate goal is for community members to meet annually at users group meetings. These are enormously profitable events, as all of us know from having attended Comdex and other conferences. Exhibit space is sold for a pretty penny; admission fees rake in the big dollars; and the seminar texts can be recorded and sold as well. Then there are sponsorship fees—what would we do without lanyards, mugs, pens, memo pads, and the like adorned with the logos of Cisco, IBM, Intel, Dell, Epson, and the like. Wikipedia and Second Life hold users group meetings, and they have been well attended. But that's a six-revenue-channel moneymaker down the road, and a goal worth striving for, once an online community is in the million-plus member category.

Sponsorships: The customary media economic model includes the "Powered by . . ." sponsorship on the community's home page. It is believed that every major vendor of cameras, video systems, and services will want to purchase a link on Calamitytower.com's home page.

Affiliate Ad Network: Calamitytower.com will build ad and sponsorship networks of affiliate partner web sites that link to the "Powered by . . ." sponsors. Important events will be rebroadcast on TV and the sponsors will pay the TV CPM rate. The community can charge the advertisers for the integration service. For video ads, the CPM is $30 to $70 and for display ads in the range of $1 to $5.

TV and Web Content Revenue: TV, radio, and newspapers are dying for interesting content and advertising. And to bring the eyeballs to the members of Calamitytower.com to TV, radio, and newspapers, the community will develop both television and web-formatted programming. As the communities' more interesting activities are ported to conventional media, the sponsorships and ads go with it. The online community newsletter will announce that significant events in the community will be broadcast on such-and-such channel, and members will turn on their TVs, or listen to their radios or buy newspapers on that particular day.

Online communities that will have the greatest ability to leverage this revenue channel are those that deal with newsworthy topics, such as rethos.com, which exposes false advertising, false political statements, and so on, thepoint.com, Angieslist.com, and projectagape.com, among others. Calamitytower.com could be in that category: compelling news coupled with a passionate membership.

Setting Up a Not-for-Profit: Calamitytower.com will set up a not-for-profit running alongside the main community, where grant money can be raised, and the grant money used to solve the pain of people voted on by the community as most in need of disaster preparedness, such as in Darfur and Chad. Contributors will be provided with links on the not-for-profit's web site.

Subscription Monthly Newsletter: The newsletter is a "glue asset," something that creates loyalty and a passion among members in the community. In it will be stories about how members achieved certain things of relevance to protect their community. There will be a Watch Us Grow page in the newsletter where regions of the country are pitted against one another to see which one can grow the most members the fastest. Good journalism will be rewarded in yet another revenue channel, the tip jar. And wolves in sheep's clothing—that is, corporate employees posing as unaffiliated, in order to promote their brands—will be outed in the newsletter. Two dollars a month is a reasonable price.

Review, Rate, and Recommend: This revenue channel is going to be one of Calamitytower.com's biggest moneymakers. There are corporations, government agencies, and enterprises that will be very curious about the conversations held in this online community. For instance, camera manufacturers, toxic chemical producers, firearms manufacturers, the Department of Homeland Security, the FBI, the CIA, and others will pay handsomely to learn what the community is talking about. Communities such as Sermo have begun selling the anonymized conversations of their members to corporations on a monthly, quarterly, and annual basis. They can be run through linguistic-based search engines such as Cognition to disambiguate confusion, and organized into research papers with graphs, bar charts, and bullet points, and command prices upward of $10,000 per study. Pfizer, Johnson & Johnson, and the like pay these sums to Sermo.com, the physicians' online community.

Glue Factors

Calamitytower.com will provide every member with a locker. And in that locker will be stored their stories, their videos, their kudos, and other tchotchkes associated with being a passionate member.

Members will be paid for bringing in handfuls of new members who remain in the group.

Members will be rewarded for their videos of members participating in regional or local get-togethers that can be uploaded to YouTube to create more visibility and awareness for the community.

There will be a registration splash page, where members will provide their profiles, project thumbnails, to explain why they have been drawn to the community—their passion if you will—and their links.

Members' votes will be tallied and stored so that the members can recall how they voted and can see how other members voted.

Alerts: Members will indicate to the community managers when they want to be alerted. For instance, if the community moderator in Kalamazoo has negotiated an agreement with the superintendent of schools to monitor hallways and doors, and the local TV station wants to televise the event, many Kalamazoo members will want to be alerted.

And finally, Calamitytower.com will have an instant reporting mobile app to capture events that are of significant importance to

EXHIBIT 8.2   Calamitytower.com Cash Flow Statement Projections: Year One

($000s)	Mo. 1	Mo. 2	Mo. 3	Mo. 4	Mo. 5	Mo. 6	Mo. 7	Mo. 8	Mo. 9	Mo. 10	Mo. 11	Mo. 12	Total Yr. 1
Members Cum.	-	-	1,000	5,000	8,000	12,000	16,000	20,000	24,000	28,000	32,000	36,000	36,000
Revenues:													
Newsletter	-	-	-	-	-	-	-	40	48	156	64	72	280
Sponsors	-	-	-	-	6	8	22	27	48	56	84	94	345
Tip-Jar	-	-	-	-	5	-	5	5	8	8	8	10	49
Affiliate Net	-	-	-	-	-	-	-	-	-	-	-	14	14
Recommend	-	-	-	-	5	5	10	10	20	20	30	30	140
Total Revenues	-	-	-	-	16	13	37	82	124	140	186	220	828
Optg. Expenses:													
Commty Build.	50	-	50	15	15	15	15	15	15	15	15	15	235
Servers	-	-	20	-	-	-	-	-	-	-	-	-	20
Systems Engs.	20	24	26	28	30	32	34	34	34	34	34	45	375
SEO, e-mktg.	-	-	-	10	15	20	25	30	35	40	60	65	300
Telecom	5	5	5	5	5	5	10	10	10	10	10	10	90
Misc. Prof.	-	-	5	5	5	5	5	5	5	5	5	5	50
Total Optg. Expenses	75	29	106	63	70	77	89	94	89	104	124	140	1070
Net Optg. Income	(75)	(29)	(106)	(63)	(54)	(64)	(25)	(12)	(35)	36	62	80	(224)[a]

[a]The first year cash deficit peaks at $428,000 in month 8. To be safe, Calamitytower.com should begin with $500,000 of angel capital.

EXHIBIT 8.2 (*Continued*) Calamitytower.com Cash Flow Statement Projections: Year Two

($000s)	Mo. 13	Mo. 14	Mo. 15	Mo. 16	Mo. 17	Mo. 18	Mo. 19	Mo. 20	Mo. 21	Mo. 22	Mo. 23	Mo. 24	Total Yr. 2
Members Cum.	40,000	44,000	48,000	52,000	56,000	60,000	64,000	68,000	72,000	76,000	80,000	84,000	84,000
Revenues:													
Newsletter	80	88	96	104	112	120	128	136	144	152	160	168	1,488
Sponsors	10	11	16	17	18	23	29	30	32	39	41	43	309
Tip Jar	10	10	10	12	12	12	14	14	14	16	16	16	156
Affiliate Net	'	'	19	'	23	23	'	'	27	'	'	31	99
Recommend	30	30	30	40	40	40	40	50	50	100	60	60	540
Total Revenues	130	139	171	173	182	218	221	230	267	267	277	318	2,592
Optg. Expenses:													
Commty Build.	15	15	15	15	15	15	15	15	15	15	15	15	180
Servers	20	'	'	'	'	'	'	'	'	'	'	'	20
Systems Engs.	48	51	54	57	60	63	66	69	72	75	78	81	774
SEO, e-mktg.	65	65	65	65	65	65	65	65	65	65	65	65	780
Telecom	15	15	15	15	15	15	18	18	18	18	18	18	198
Misc. Prof.	6	6	6	6	6	6	7	7	7	7	7	7	76
Total Optg. Expenses	165	152	155	173	161	164	171	174	177	180	186	186	2,028
Net Optg. Income	(35)	(13)	16	'	21	54	50	56	87	87	91	132	564

the community. This is especially important in local communities or in review, rank, and recommend communities, where a false advertisement or an untruthful statement by a government official can be reported live and with a video shown to the entire community when it occurs.

Business Plan

The two-year cash flow statement projections of Calamitytower.com are shown in Exhibit 8.2.

Summary

It will take a few years to see and feel the efforts of these two community-based businesses. But they will succeed, because all of the technology is in place. Moreover, we are each of us wired to collaborate and to cooperate in order to solve problems. Most of the online community and mobile social network start-ups will be devoted to solving pain in the five big areas that interest people on a personal level—to be more popular (for young people), create more wealth, be more attractive, be healthier, have a better sex life, and create a larger estate for our grandchildren (for older people). But when these fields become very crowded and lead to losses, then a handful of heroic social network entrepreneurs will slap on their six-guns, saddle up their broncos, and set about terminating global warming and foiling terrorism and local catastrophes. Do you have the guts to take on Churchillian problems of this magnitude? If you do, you may become one of the planet's great heroes.

When you boil it down, social networking, as I said in the opening sentence of this book, is all about bringing intelligent people together and getting them to exchange ideas. Collaborating leads to solving common problems. Disrupting rapacious corporations and government agencies that don't care whose lives they trample on. Bringing truthfulness to markets in order to lower prices and improve efficiencies. These are some of the goals of online communities founders, who will take on the enormous challenges of global warming and terrorism. You will not be able to accomplish this by spending day after day in front of your computer trying to persuade strategic alliance partners, owners of important brands, angel capitalists, and others to help you. The stories I told in the earlier chapters of this book about Curtis Carlson, whose wife dressed up like a majorette and danced in grocery stores to encourage the use of Gold Bond Stamps; Roy Park, who persuaded mayors to hold Duncan Hines days to stimulate interest in a cake mix; and Sam Shoen, who visited hundreds of gas stations to convince their owners to create space for trailers and do all the paperwork for his new U-Haul System, were meant to encourage you to get off your butts and meet with people who can be helpful to you in launching your social networks.

Bibliography

Barnfather, Maurice. "Capital Formation." *Forbes*, March 29, 1982.

Benkler, Yochai. *The Wealth of Networks*. New Haven: Yale University Press, 2006.

Berlin, Isaiah. *Personal Impressions*. New York: Viking, 1981.

Bowe, Christopher. "Media Clicking on to Sermo." *Financial Times*, October 15, 2007.

Brown, Patricia Leigh. "For EcoMoms, Saving Earth Begins at Home." *New York Times*, February 16, 2008.

Garcia, Francisco. "Illuminating the Obscure Model Called Fair Isaac." Anderson School of Management, UCLA, October, 2006.

Getzel, Jacob, and Mihály, Csikszentmihalyi. *The Creative Vision: A Longitudinal Study of Problem Finding in Art*. New York: John Wiley & Sons, 1976.

Gilder, George. *The Spirit of Enterprise*. New York: Simon & Schuster, 1984.

Gilmore, James H., and B. Joseph Pine II. *Authenticity: What Consumers Really Want*. Cambridge: Harvard Business School Press, 2007.

Goetz, Thomas. "Online Communities for the Chronically Ill." *New York Times*, March 23, 2008.

Harford, Tim. *The Logic of Life*. New York: Random House, 2008.

———. *The Undercover Economist*. New York: Random House, 2007.

Jacob, H.E. *Six Thousand Years of Bread*. New York: Skyhorse Publishing, 2007.

Levy, Steven. *The Perfect Thing: How the iPOD Shuffles Commerce, Culture and Cookies*. New York: Simon & Schuster, 2006.

List, John A. "Does Market Experience Eliminate Market Anomalies." *Quarterly Journal of Economics* 118 (2003).

Mamet, David. *Glengarry Glen Ross*. New York: Grove Press, 1984.

McCraw, Thomas K. *Prophet of Innovation: Joseph Schumpeter and Creative Destruction*. Cambridge: Harvard University Press, 2007.

McGregor, Jena. "Consumer Vigilantes." *Business Week*, March 3, 2008.

Milne, John. "The Entrepreneur." *Business New Hampshire*, August 1984.

Perkins, D.N. *The Mind's Best Work*. Cambridge: Harvard University Press, 1981.

Pink, Daniel H. *A Whole New Mind*. New York: Riverhead Books, 2005.

Rasmussen, Andrea, and Carolyn Ude. "Kevin George: Unilever's Digital Media Strategy." *Strategy Business*. October 19, 2007.

Silver David. *Smart Start-Ups: How Entrepreneurs and Corporations Can Profit by Starting Online Communities*. Hoboken, N.J.: John Wiley & Sons, New York, 2007.

Story Louise. "The New Advertising Outlet: Your Life." *New York Times*. October 14, 2007.

Stross, Randall. "From 10 Hours a Week, $10 Million a Year. *New York Times*, January 13, 2008.

Index